Endorsements

"Love is the cornerstone, no matter what faith or spiritual path you're on. And, in this beautifully written book, we journey with Chris, who shares his life experiences from childhood to his years as an Evangelical minister, in the most authentic, loving way. Many people will see themselves and relate—hopefully finding comfort in knowing they are not alone—allowing for healing to take place. Anyone who is involved with Evangelicals, by association, will value this book for the insights and education it provides. And, for those who are part of the movement of which Chris writes, if read with an open mind and heart, it has the potential to be transforming".

—Rev. Michele Sevacko, PhD

"Chris Kratzer lances the festering boil that is much of modern evangelical Christianity. Leatherbound Terrorism is shocking and embarrassing and fantastically liberating. Thank you, Holy Spirit, for Kratzer, for his journey, for his courage. No, for his honesty, for setting the joy of Jesus before him and never letting him settle for our American religious skubula. For all those sisters and brothers who know better, who have always known better and refused to drink the Kool Aid, but had nowhere to go, this is your book. Now, let's get to work rethinking everything we thought we knew in the light of Jesus. I am in."

—C. Baxter Kruger, Ph.D.,
Author of the international best seller,
The Shack Revisited, and Patmos

"When the word "disruptor" is used in the business world, it refers to forward-thinking, innovative, ambitious models that disrupt the status quo, usually in a good way. Those companies and people are usually applauded inside that context. When the word is used in the church world, it's a different story. Disruptors in the church world are seen as rebellious and unorthodox, as irritants to the established system. History, on the other hand, often looks favorably upon them. Think Martin Luther, the Apostle Paul or even Jesus, Himself.

Chris Kratzer is a disruptor. When it comes to his assessment of the 21st Century Evangelical Church and its surrounding culture, I frequently found myself internally shouting, "Yes! Go, Chris!" Then, to be honest, there are things he says that cause me to sometimes find myself thinking, 'Nuh-uh. No way. What are you thinking?' And then I have to think about what he said again. Sometimes, I still don't agree, but, at other times, I find myself having to admit that he's right and I'm forced to repent and press the reset button on my own viewpoint about the matter. In other words, Chris makes me think, a practice often discouraged in the legalistic culture of the Evangelical world. One thing I like much about Chris is that he doesn't parrot anybody. Not on the left or the right. He brings Raw Grace right out into the open and demands that we figure out how to justify our attitudes and actions in light of that Presence. He insists that we reexamine views we have held sacred and he does it in a compelling way.

Leatherbound Terrorism is going to get a rise out of you. That I promise. It will put a compassionate lump in your throat as you read about Chris' background. Depending on your existing viewpoints, it will either excite you to see a man speak so boldly about controversial subjects, or it will annoy you because of the things he says. But, make no mistake about it, we need people like Kratzer and books like this. They add value to the ongoing discussion about these matters by making us think about them and then rethink them again. Some people are going to love this book. Some are going to hate it. But I predict one thing: Many are going to talk about it and read it, and no small number will find themselves being changed as a result."

—Steve McVey
Best-selling author

"For too long, Evangelical Christianity has been mired in exclusionary tactics, both theological and political. Because of this, the Church is limping along, perpetually hellbent on kicking to the curb, any and all who dare question their so-called "correct doctrines." Chris Kratzer was one of these. In Leatherbound Terrorism, Kratzer chronicles his journey, all the while, orienting his readers to the one thing that saved his faith: Grace. Indeed, this book is a wake-up call to any who profess themselves as an Evangelical Christian."

—Matthew J. Distefano, Author of 4 books,
Blogs at Patheos.com,
One of three co-hosts of the
Heretic Happy Hour podcast

LEATHERBOUND
TERRORISM

Crucified By Conservative Evangelicalism,

Resurrected By Jesus

LEATHERBOUND
TERRORISM

Crucified By Conservative Evangelicalism,

Resurrected By Jesus

CHRIS KRATZER

LEATHERBOUND **TERRORISM**
Crucified By Conservative Evangelicalism, Resurrected By Jesus

ISBN-10: 0692191623

ISBN-13: 978- 0692191620 (Grace Publishing)

Printed in the United States of America.

Book Cover Design By: Harrison Kratzer, www.harrisonkratzer.com

Book Edited / Formatted By: Beverly Dobrich, Living Leaves LLC

Table of Contents

In Dedication

To my wife, Amy: When God thought about how best to love me, He made you. We have taken this journey, we are this journey, together—beautiful. Every word, sentence, and page lives because of the strength and splendor of who you are and who we are, inseparably.

To Harrison, Cailyn, Madelyn, and Ashton: May the words of these pages envelop you in Grace and bring meaning and light to your path. As you so richly bless me as a father, may they long bless you, forever.

To Michael Hailey: You are the father I never had, and the pastor I never deserved. The most pivotal, life-giving transitions in my ministry have all centered around your influence. I write because you saw it in me to do so. May these words bring honor to you and your legacy.

To Amy Harrison: As the very first person to befriend and financially support my writing ministry, I am deeply thankful. This book happens because you believed in me, first.

To Baxter Kruger: Your tenacity of belief in me, my writing, and the story I have to tell has authored the courage in me to cross the finish line of this book. You turned my reluctancy into resolve. I am deeply thankful beyond words.

To Nancy Manno: Thank you for willingness to demand I show up fully and completely in the words of this book. Your gift is priceless to me.

To all my supporters and Facebook family: You are the bravery, Grace, and love that inspires me. My deepest thanks, love, and appreciation to all of you. This book is for you.

FOREWORD

Most forewords are written by another published or accomplished author and for good reason. However, let me say right off, that's not me! I am writing this foreword for two reasons.

First, because outside his family, I probably know this author as well (or better) than anyone. And, secondly, because Chris Kratzer is not only my friend; Chris is also like my son. A son that I admire. A son that makes me proud. A son "in whom I am well pleased."

I met Chris some 20 years ago, as a young idealistic minister with stars in his eyes. He was deeply determined to reach thousands of people with the message of Evangelical Christianity, and, in the process, build a mega church to minister to all those who were reached. Or at least, that's the story men like Chris, myself and countless others continue to tell ad infinitum, ad nauseam.

So, 20 years ago, this young, wide-eyed Pastor walks into my life. He had just planted a new church in the Tampa Bay area and had driven down to our church for one of our services on a Friday night. Chris told me he was interested in learning some things about growing a casual and contemporary church like ours and wondered if he could "hang out" with us every so often.

It wasn't long before Chris was a regular around our church. Every chance he had, he was there learning, asking questions, studying and soaking up everything he could. He sat in on staff meetings, we went to lunches together, I even baptized him and his wife one Sunday morning.

Now, I will spare you the details of what happened in the years that followed for Chris and his family. You will read about them in this incredibly raw and passionately written book. But I will say that the man I began to know 20 years ago is not the same man I know today.

The young man I knew back then with the "stars in his eyes" about the church and, particularly, the evangelical church, has morphed into this amazingly mature, compassionate man who's sole desire is to share with others…the amazing grace of God; the kind of grace that has no strings attached. The kind of grace that includes everyone, and excludes NO ONE! The kind of grace Chris not only discovered, but the kind of grace that he lives every day of his life.

By the way, some of the books you read will stretch you. Some will inspire you. Some will make you angry and challenge everything you hold dear. This book you hold in your hands will do all those things, I guarantee you. And, as an added bonus, this book will mess you up…but in the most WONDERFUL sort of way.

If you have grown disillusioned about faith and God, about the church and Christianity, you are not alone. If you have grown weary of the message of condemnation and have grown tired of going to church only to hear about how terrible you are and how God is just not pleased with you, then you really need to read this book. If you have ever been mistreated, abused, shunned, ridiculed, given up on…you must READ THIS BOOK!

Recently, I was speaking on how to overcome our fears when I made this statement: "Often times our most overwhelming fear…is the fear of letting go, letting go of a habit, a relationship, a job, a dream or even an entire way of life and living."

Chris Kratzer has become a virtual master at "letting go." He is one of the bravest men I know. And I pray you, too, become brave as you read his real, raw and incredibly beautiful story.

Pastor Michael Hailey, New Day Church

The first thing that grows out of a heart captivated by Grace is Honesty, the next is Love—

Unconditional and Unrestrained.

INTRODUCTION

We're not face to face, so these words must serve the hope of connecting my heart to yours.

There's a lot I really want to say, and even more that I hope you will hear. I'm going to shoot straight from the hip, right from the start, I hope you don't mind. There are stories of truth, and then, there are true stories. This book is both--a tapestry of words—revealing my awakening.

Trust me, I'm not trying to convince you, shame you, or change your mind. My heart truly cares and is filled with understanding, respect, and compassion. I only desire to give you the kind of clarity that can be useful. So, along the way, if you can't say "amen," perhaps you can say, "ouch," or maybe just "yeesh," all of which would be understandable. Besides, I don't write with a priority to convince—that's the job of the Spirit. Rather, mine is primarily a voice of solidarity for and with the religiously oppressed, that they might know they are valued, loved, and heard.

That said, those who know me (as you soon will), recognize beyond all doubt that I've changed—nearly everything about me. I'm a different person, now, having traveled a complete one-eighty in beliefs, values, faith, heart, and my sense of self and purpose. By some, this onset of change has been met with their glares of disapproval and anxiety. Perhaps, to them, it feels like it's happened overnight, but I can assure you, as you will read, it's been a long time coming.

Regardless, the truth is, I've stepped away and outside of the conservative Evangelical faith I once held so closely. Twenty years of being a committed conservative Evangelical pastor, no less. You'll get the backstory in the chapters ahead, but the simple truth is this: my mind has been changed and my heart has outgrown the beliefs to which I once subscribed—not in some kind of arrogant way that renders me better than another, only different.

I've never been good at silencing my conscience and avoiding the onset of what I believe to be undeniable truth. I wasn't expecting it, I wasn't looking for it. In fact, nothing can be more unwelcomed in life than change—especially the kind that costs nearly everything. Beyond my control and outside of my desires, through a series of profound experiences which will be unfolded in this book, the Father, Son, and Holy Spirit, in inseparable concert with One Another, confronted me with the ultimate question of my conservative Evangelicalism, "What if you're wrong?"

What if you've been deceived? What if all that you hold to be so true and life-giving isn't so true and life-giving after all? What if the default settings of your faith are in fact ladened with faults and set with fallacy? What if all that you have never dared to truly question should have been truly questioned a long time ago? What if the life you think you have embraced is truly no life at all? What if you've missed Jesus, the Spirit, and God's desires completely?

That burning bush of retrospection, set ablaze by a series of divine events and inquisitions, has served to bring perhaps the most confronting moments in all my life. With every step of divine wrestling, I knew deep within my being, if I was honest, the confession that God was pressing out of me was that I wasn't just wrong, I was completely lost. In fact, having not only bit the conservative Evangelical apple, but spending nearly a lifetime trying to climb the tree, I was thrust into moments where there was essentially no other honest choice but to see that I had not only been duped and deceived, but conservative Evangelical Christianity had left me a skeleton-of-a-person having wasted so much of my life.

I know all that may be hard to hear, but that's the truth that must be revealed if there is to be any chance of freedom for you or for me.

In that way, at times, this may taste like a harsh book, but, if this is going to be an honest book that presents the clarity that we all need, it will have moments that may sting, not because that's my intention or desire, but because of the heights from which conservative Evangelicalism has truly fallen from Grace.

In fact, if you feel compelled along this journey to tone-police my words, perhaps you would consider that it's not the choice of my words that is truly alarming, but the necessity of them. Trust me, this journey has been far harder to write than I expect it could ever be to read. But what am I supposed to do when everything in my being knows this may be the most important revelation being wielded on the planet? A revelation that can't break the chains of religious oppression and deception without accuracy, even if it's difficult, at times, to stomach.

Every baptism begins with a drowning.

The sacred waters are ready, are you?

"A simple, childlike faith in a Divine Friend solves all the problems that come to us by land or sea"
—Helen Keller, My Religion

CHAPTER ONE
A Fish Named Jesus

Where did I first meet Jesus? The hospital, of course.

I was seven years old and suffering from severe asthma. A few days prior, during a crystal cold, snow-covered winter's evening in Brookfield, Wisconsin, I awoke in the middle of the night without the capacity to breathe. It felt like my lungs had been shrink-wrapped and my throat clamped by iron fists. No, it wasn't the first time, but we all had hoped a new medication would have prevented this. With pre-calculated steps that had been rehearsed before, my parents swiftly gathered me into the back seat of our brown station wagon as there was no time nor path for an ambulance. I knew as I lay there navigating my balance through the frantic turns of my dad's driving, that my only chance of survival was to override every urge welling up within me to surrender to sheer panic. Upon arrival and a slippery jog through an icy, snow-drifted parking lot in the arms of my father, a police officer joined us in the elevator to assure our speedy travel. Somehow, we bi-passed the emergency room and went directly to the fifth floor which had become my home away from home.

For some reason, I wasn't gifted with a healthy childhood. Though my parents were certainly people of good heart, there was physical and emotional darkness waiting around every corner. Some of which resulted from physical causes beyond their control, but others rose up from much more diabolical sources. From birth, it was clear I was different. My skin was festered with eczema, my weight was lacking, and my esophagus barely wide enough to swallow food. One of the first memories I can recall is of a sterile surgical room where a doctor forced a carrot-like rubber apparatus down my throat where it would stay for several weeks to enlarge my ability to swallow.

I suspect it wasn't by chance that during every asthmatic visit to the hospital, they positioned me in the same room with the same bed closest to the same window and nearest to the nurse's station. There were other beds, but no other children. The floors were cold, the beds covered with white linens. Only the walls fashioned a tan finish. Yet, my eyes always focused on the one and only television hanging in the corner just above an outlooking window. During the nights, I found that rocking back and forth upon my bed while crouched on top of my knees as I chatter, my teeth gave me a comfort I needed.

After a frantic rush of doctors and nurses with tubes, needles, IV bags, and a mask, my breathing was restored for a time. With the raw senses of a child without a childhood, I knew it was a highly dangerous situation that could change at any moment, even though that reality was urgently trying to be disguised by the smiles of doctors and nurses. The medical contraptions keeping me alive restricted my sleep to an upward position; there would be no rocking back and forth that night. Yet, the morning to follow would prove to be a special day.

When I first awoke, the television was already on. Not just on, but dialed into my favorite show. Sesame Street always had a way of taking my attention to places it needed to go. Yet this time, it was as if one of the characters approached the screen, looked me in the eyes, and spoke to me directly. The figure was not familiar to me nor the tone of his voice. I can't remember exactly what was said, but I knew in a way like never before, I was not alone. In fact, whoever was speaking called me by name. I could hardly believe it or contain my surprise. That evening, my father stopped by for a visit after a long day at work. Even before he could free himself of his wet winter clothing, I excitedly spoke of this amazing experience. In fact, the more he politely insisted of the impossibility, the more I was convinced that there could have been no mistaking what had occurred on the screen. Evidently, dad wasn't going to discuss it further, and mom wouldn't dare harbor an opposing view. Perhaps, however, a nurse might be able to bring clarity and deeper understanding to what had transpired that morning.

Finally, when the coast was clear, and my family had exited the scene, there was one last nurse I knew who would arrive to give me my evening medicine. I certainly wish I could remember her name, and even more, her appearance. For me, I always seemed to remember the tongue-assaulting tastes of medicines and the uncomfortable feelings of procedures, more than the people doing them. But this time, nothing could erase the words she replied to my questions about the television. Without hesitancy or waver in her voice, she suggested, "Perhaps that was Jesus coming to make you brave."

Soon, the room wasn't so cold, the hospital smells weren't so profound, and the fears lingering within were subdued of their gravity. Jesus had personally come to be with me, and His bravery was now mine. Nobody could unhinge me from this conviction, it was a transfusion of divine assurance into the marrow of my soul, reviving everything that was being put to death.

A couple days later, when my breathing returned to normal, the morning came for my hospital discharge. There's a vulnerability and weakness I felt each time upon returning to "normal." It isn't easy going back into a world where one moment everything is fine and the next you're gasping for air, gauging your distance from an inhaler and vigorously calculating whether you can take another dose. Compared to hospital life, it might seem to be a welcomed reality to the untrained eye, but returning home wasn't without a sure heightening of anxiety, for many reasons.

So, perhaps having read between the lines, to send me off with an extra boost of encouragement, the nurses filled an IV bag with goldfish for my journey home. Just a few moments before, being wheeled down to the hospital entrance where my dad waited with the family car, I paused for a moment as I gazed upon my new friends swimming around. There was one that caught my eye and seemed altogether different. After a quick glance back at that television, now behind me, and with an emerging grin on my face, I decided to name that one "Jesus" to make sure He would come with me and so would His bravery.

What I didn't know then is what I surely know now, how that first encounter with God would forever shape me. For this is the Jesus who is Grace, whose beauty and expanse enveloped my entire seven-year-old being. Whose light, power, and goodness are otherworldly. The One who shows up in your life long before He shows up in a Bible or a service. Through whatever means is meaningful, even a goldfish or a television screen. The Jesus who brings Himself into your world with one song and one heartbeat, to infuse in you a bravery to embrace all that is good and face all that is not. A bravery that loves you without expectation or reciprocation, and refuses to harbor malice or disappointment as He gazes without restriction upon your everything. The Jesus who forever and always sees you as a child simply trying to find your way, with the satisfaction and assurance of One who holds all things, especially you, forever and always.

This is the Jesus I know, who bends his heart towards the broken, whose smile cannot be dissuaded. The one who cannot help but love when love is what is least expected. The One whose Grace is entirely and thoroughly sufficient—without disclaimers, fine print, or pre-qualification. This is the Jesus whose light transcends every sunrise and renders void every darkening hell.

With a compassion that leaves no room for condemnation. With a love that leaves no room for conditions. With a Grace that leaves no room for

28

religion. With a heaven that leaves no room for punishment. With a freedom that leaves no room for imprisonment. With an image that leaves no room for pretending. With an affirmation that leaves no room for discrimination, and with His mind given to each of us that connects us all in Him and the entire universe together—this is the Jesus I know.

This is the Jesus who met me at just seven years old, who came just because He could. The One who collided my life with Himself, making both indistinguishable.

This is the Jesus whose Grace and bravery would save me from a future that was soon to unfold.

"Shame isn't a quiet grey cloud, shame is a drowning man who claws his way on top of you, scratching and tearing your skin, pushing you under the surface."—Kirsty Eagar, Raw Blue

CHAPTER TWO
The Drowning

With hospital visits every couple months, it was all I could do to tread water. Yet, at the end of the day, I was surviving. I was making it through while trying to cling to some semblance of a childhood.

I learned to manage the anxiety, sleepless nights, hospital stays, and constant need for vigilance. Like Linus with his blanket, he knows it stinks, but at least there is some comfort in its familiarity. More and more, I could handle the asthma and learn to live with it as my companion.

Yet, the waters of asthma weren't the only tide seeking to consume me. My lungs weren't the only organs inflamed with anxiety. My entire skin soon began to tell the tale of a childhood filled with trauma.

Eczema found its way into nearly every part of my body. I would scratch my hands to the point of bleeding and had enough steroids pumped into my body to significantly stunt my growth. The kids at school made fun of me and the red sores constantly breaking out everywhere. In fact, my nickname was "cracker," because of all the cracks in my skin. With allergies constantly devouring me, I was seldom allowed to play outside with my classmates. Every day was a battle to subdue the symptoms that created a living nightmare of insecurity and potential death. I was a child learning to gaze at the world through the narrow lens of survival and a mind preoccupied with death and the disapproval of others.

Leatherbound **Terrorism**

Sadly, during those rare moments where life seemed to normalize, my breathing opened wide, my eczema subsided, and I was free to laugh, play, and explore as a child, another lion roared in the wings waiting to devour me. Just when a fresh wind of hope breezed my way, the ominous clouds of another evil quickly emerged to darken the atmosphere once again.

As best I can remember, it started out as a perfectly sunny summer day. As I had before, I traveled on my bike up and around the corner to a friend's house to play. She was cute, I can't deny. And better yet, she knew of my childhood struggles, at least the physical ones. Jamie and I were friends, both navigating our way through early childhood.

It was unusual for one of my sisters to join in our play, perhaps because of the age difference. Yet somehow, on that day, we all found ourselves in the backyard of a home we rarely visited. Their kids were older, and our paths usually didn't cross. In fact, on this occasion, they weren't even home, no one was. Despite the weirdness of it all, there we were, me, my friend Jamie, some other kids, and one of my sisters. Seemingly out of nowhere, the topic of love came up and so did our relationship. Jamie and I spent a lot of time playing together in the neighborhood, so perhaps they thought we were a childhood couple of some kind. With a bit of teasing and pressure, the crowd of kids that joined my sister began to ask, "Do you guys like each other?" At eight years old, what were we supposed to say? Yet, the more we didn't have an answer, the more pressing they became. There were trees around and several bushes, which seemed to become the perfect setup for their next move. Having made a kind of circle around us, one of the kids suggested, "If you like each other so much, then get on top of each other naked." What started as a topic of laughter and childhood silliness soon turned to a level of seriousness Jamie and I didn't know how to squelch. Within moments, somehow we ended up taking off our clothes, and doing just exactly as they said. I can clearly remember the wind blowing through the trees and the feeling of a new level of innocence being swept up along with it.

Sadly, this wasn't the first time. Our home had several floors including a basement with a kind of split-level design. One of my sisters had a bedroom near the entrance to the basement stairway. I'm not sure exactly how the moment came into being, but I can picture it well. It was a small room with a window that looked out just above the ground. The walls were dark and a bunk bed covered one side of the room. Once again, there I was, lying naked on top of one my sisters on the lower bed. A few seconds past, and then my mom unexpectedly opened the door to see what had transpired in full view. What was perhaps most surprising is that she didn't say a word and simply closed the door to go back to whatever she was doing.

That was just the beginning of a vicious cycle of increasing sexual abuse what would last for years to come. In fact, much later into my adulthood when I learned to confront my past and deal with a childhood of sexual abuse, I finally mustered the courage to tell my parents of all that had happened, hoping to find that they were innocently oblivious. Upon returning home for a family visit during my third year in Seminary, at the advice of a counselor I had been seeing, I waited for the perfect moment to disclose the sexual abuse of my childhood. Both were sitting opposite each other reading the newspaper and enjoying an evening drink. I entered the family room that was lit with the early evening sun. I sat in a comfortable chair nearby and began with small talk. Nothing I said seemed to be enough to warrant their attention as their faces didn't move from behind what they were reading. With a moment of sudden courage, I spoke thoroughly, specifically, and directly about the sexual abuse I had endured, often repeating myself. Still to this day, I can't put words to the silence of their response. There were no questions, comments, or moments of clarification. They didn't even pause to look me in the eye to acknowledge my voice. Nothing was said, absolutely nothing. It was literally as if I had simply spoken about something as trivial as tomorrow's weather.

Leatherbound **Terrorism**

After waiting and waiting some more, I arose out of my chair with a newfound awareness of the darkness that must have truly been. Perhaps, my inner child knew it all along, and that was the root cause of a childhood gasping for breath. My father once saved my life during an asthma attack, but now there was a shadow upon it all. In fact, memories I once sterilized of their venom were now revealed of their poison. Yet, believe it or not, sexual abuse wasn't the only claw suffocating my breath, there was even more--much more.

In that same house, my room was just up the stairs from the main floor. From the top of the steps, I could barely begin to see the mantle to our fireplace in the main family room below. One evening, my parents were fighting. About what, I'm not exactly sure. This was a weekly event at the very least, my dad was quite temperamental. Sometimes his rage was directed toward my oldest sister's rebellion, but mostly towards my mother. I was asleep upstairs when the familiar sounds of shouting emerged. This time, there was something different in the air. I awoke and tiptoed out from my room to take a few steps down the stairs. What came into view was a horrible horror of surprise. My father had tied up my mother with rope to subdue her on the couch with tape over her mouth. This was the same couch upon which we huddled for family devotions to learn about Jesus. This was the same couch from which my conservative Christian father would hope to instill within us a sense of morals and Godly character. Upon seeing my gaze around a corner, my father's explanation was to insist to me that mom was, "out of control." One moment we're learning stories from the Bible in front of the fire, the next we're wondering if we're going to survive a home of unpredictable violence. I returned to my bed with a pit in my stomach and a visual I had no idea how to process.

Thankfully, my father never directed his rage towards me. Instead, he had other methods. In fact, when I was ten, we moved to Florida where, surprisingly, my asthma and eczema quickly dissipated. Within a few months, I was completely free from all my medicines. Finally, I was able to begin a childhood that for a long time was largely constricted. Yet, in my father's eyes, my new found freedom from illness meant there would be no more excuses for any lack of academic performance. Apparently, that was his big takeaway.

Even though our move to Florida was a great improvement for our family as a whole, my father remained a stern, easily angered man. I quickly learned that he had strong expectations for everyone and a temperamental impatience. It was not uncommon for him to engage in "car fights" with other drivers who weren't meeting his desires for speed or moving out of the way. It seemed as if we all lived on the edge of my father's mood. One moment, the horizon was filled with sunshine, the next, a crashing storm. Was he bipolar? I think not. Rather, I suspect he was a man haunted by deep levels of pain that he never learned to navigate. His was a generation of subdued emotions and psychological denial, particularly for males. In reading letters he wrote to my mother while they were dating, he was a troubled soul who despised rejection and feverishly needed to feel in control.

Yet, no matter how much I might be able to explain it and blanket his behavior with compassion, I refuse to excuse it or dismiss its impact. For the person I needed to become to survive was not always a pure one.

I wasn't an expert at forging report cards, but I quickly learned how. During one of his many "motivational" lectures, my father once cornered me in his room with a stern voice saying, "If you get a "c" on your report card that means you're average, and Kratzers aren't average." I understood the parental concern, but, even greater, internalized the pressure. In fact, at the end of my first year in middle school, I knew I had done poorly in both math and science. My mind quickly raced ahead to figure out a way to dodge the bullet I knew would be fired. After several brainstorms to find a way out, I realized my best option was to forge the report card that I knew was forthcoming. It would arrive in the mail, so I would have to somehow commandeer it before my parents did. Every day for the first weeks of summer, I anxiously waited for the mail to arrive with my heart beating out of my chest. Luckily, it finally came, and I was able to secure it without incident. I opened it and quickly began the process of cutting out good grades from previous report cards and carefully pasting them over the bad ones. You might think that would appear to be an obvious forgery, but I got so good at it that it worked every time. Well, that is, nearly every time.

During one such forgery, there were a couple of grades I simply couldn't fix. In sheer panic, the usual process wasn't working. Despite my best efforts, on the kitchen counter sat my report card with a glaring "c" that I knew would usher in my doom most assuredly. Let's just say, when my father arrived home from work, he wasn't happy--not happy at all. I had learned early on, my best chance of survival when dad gets mad was to lay low and out of the scene. So, I stayed in my room with my ears to the door, listening carefully. I knew my father would despise my performance, and the thought of his displeasure was devastating to me. Yet, I couldn't help but wonder, "Am I such a terrible child?" What kind of life is a life that needs to be forged?

Knowing that I was upset in my room, my mother soon came to console me. I told her that, "Dad must not love me, because I got a 'c.'" She quickly corrected me, insisting I was wrong. However, I wasn't easily convinced, especially when for some time, I had seen her sneaking drinks in order to medicate herself from a broken marriage—where's the credibility in that? To resolve our disagreement, she decided it would be best for her to personally escort me to where my father was sitting in the living room and solicit him directly. Still, to this day, I can see the dim lighting in the room as I turned the corner from our kitchen to where my dad was seated in a rocking chair darkly shadowed by the moment. His tempo was slow, and his face was stern. As I stood next to her, my mother inquired of my father, "Honey, Chris doesn't think that you love him because he got a "c" on his report card. Tell him that's not true." To that my father responded without hesitation and with a determined cadence, "With grades like that, he's no son of mine."

That was it, game over.

The final blow, the nail in the coffin.

The fork in the road.

While, somehow, the asthma couldn't kill me, the eczema couldn't devour me, the sexual abuse couldn't destroy me, his words drowned me—completely.

Nine simple, calculated words.

Standing there, flashbacks fired in my brain, a thousand scenes ran through my mind. Memories of that hospital room where it all began.

This time, there were would be no IV bag full of fish to encourage me. No, this time, the IV bag was me, it was my life--trapped and drowning. There I am, swimming to stay alive with, of all people, my father pulling me to the bottom.

Nine simple, calculated words.

With no way to escape, all I could do is wonder, "Where is Jesus?"

I desperately needed saving, and so did my father.

Surely, He was with me, but where?

Surely, He could save us, but how?

He does want to save me, doesn't He?

"It is not our part to master all the tides of the world, but to do what is in us for the succour of those years wherein we are set, uprooting the evil in the fields that we know, so that those who live after may have clean earth to till. What weather they shall have is not ours to rule."—J.R.R. Tolkien, The Return of the King

CHAPTER THREE
Drinking The Poison

It was in middle school that I first began to sense a desire to become a pastor, perhaps to heal my own wounds and to assist in the healing of the same in others. I enjoyed caring for people, the power of spiritual connection, and becoming an important person in people's lives. As twisted as it may sound, from an early age, I would fantasize about the emergence of real-life, terrible situations in which I would become the hero to save the day. Somehow, the redemption of others was connected to my own. Yet, in truth, the heights of my visions of grandeur were equal to the depths of my insecurities.

For all I had been through, I can't remember a time in my youth when there wasn't a special, mystical, and deeply spiritual connection between myself and Jesus. From the time He visited me in the hospital, His presence and strength of mind never left me. Yet, deep within, I had two opposing streams raging within me. One that was flowing with a constant state of worry and anxiety, and the other, teeming over with a sense of inward bravery. As much as I believed in the goodness of Jesus, I did wonder, at times, with all that happened to me as a child, was God for me, against me, or something in- between? Perhaps it was all punishment for something deeply wrong within me that I had not yet identified. Either way, pastoral ministry seemed like the key to appeasing God, if need be, healing my childhood, saving myself, and, somehow, gaining the applause of my family. I wanted to find a purpose for my pain, and maybe even more so, a vindication from a childhood hell of never being normal. Somehow, if I could become "great" it would all have been worthwhile, and my enemies would bow in shame. Little did I know, with all these aspirations fueled by the inadequacies beneath them, I was a perfect storm in the making, a prime candidate for being seduced by the most diabolical poison ever wielded upon the earth.

After college, I spent four years in seminary, graduated, and formally became a Lutheran pastor on a Friday and married my wife on Saturday. Two weeks later, after our honeymoon, I began my formal ministry. It didn't take long to discover that for all the things I enjoyed about caring for people and helping them encounter God, there was a lot more to this "church" thing than I could ever learn in a book. My calling to be a pastor was secure and well rooted, but my questions and concerns about the realities of church-life were ever increasing. In just the first five years of ministry, I experienced unbelievable "church" challenges, a staff member barging into our home for the purpose of viciously shaming my wife, and a congregational leader literally threatening my life—to name just a few.

It was then that that allures of conservative Evangelical Christianity were pimped in my direction. It was suggested to me by people I deeply respected that the reason why my "church" experience was so unhealthy, and my ministry was filled with such challenges, was because it was all so progressively unbiblical, carnal, and contrary to the will and favor of God. They insisted that I was part of a liberal spiritual system, church philosophy, and faith understanding that God did not support nor approve. In their mind, my spiritual life was false, and my sense of God and the Christian life was misguided. That's the reason why ministry, church, and a life of peace and success were eluding me. Therefore, all I had to do was to jump ship and become a conservative Evangelical, and ministry fame, fortune, wholeness, and prosperity would be mine. My marriage, my faith, my ministry, and all of life would fall into place and be taken to the next level by joining the right team. God will do his part, but I have to do mine—that's the revelation that was missing. The whole "fish-named-

Jesus" of my childhood was true, but He required a "faithfulness-named-Chris" to close the deal and work His will.

I swallowed it, hook, line, and sinker--all pun intended.

In fact, within a few puffs and injections of its seductive creed, conservative Evangelicalism became an instant drug of choice to numb the pains of inadequacy that had long been building in the caverns of my being. Never did there appear to be a better way to appease a conditional, loving father and heal the struggles, sins, and shame of my youth than to embark on a spiritual climb designed to satisfy the ultimate conditional, loving Father—the god of conservative Evangelicalism who promised to rid me of my demons if I pressed in hard enough and learned to traverse the tightrope of conservative faith. In my mind, salvation had finally come in an Evangelical deity offering me a spiritual track upon which I could race to right my wrongs, earn value to my condemned life, and render myself lovable at the finish.

Just color within the lines, give the proper responses, think and believe the right things, fight the good fight of faith, and I, too, could become "successful" and satisfactory for Jesus. Perhaps then, both my father on earth and the Father above could finally love me—perhaps, then, even I could finally love me. The ultimate trifecta of acceptance and approval was just an Evangelical "to do" list away, all leading to a position seated high above the world upon which to feel good about myself through a subtle looking-down upon others. It was all so righteous and perfect—so it seemed.

With a snappy new Jesus-step in my shoes, I eagerly surveyed the landscape of conservative Evangelical Christianity and its heroes. They all had obvious common denominators—big churches, big book deals, big speaking schedules, big conferences, big baptismal numbers, big budgets, big leadership philosophies, big vision, and even wives with big hair. Every sermon was finely crafted with spiritual formulas, principles, and steps that lead to the "big" life. Every service was meticulously programmed for ultimate appeal and emotion. The Bible was cut and dry, people were either in or out, sin was clear and easily defined, the truth was black or white, and either you had a place at the cool pastors' lunch table or you didn't. People on the outside were seen as a project to assimilate into the inside, and then to "grow" towards ultimately partnering in the pastor's grandiose vision to "make fully devoted followers of Jesus Christ," a/k/a, "my big ass ministry ego trip." That's the truth, and it was all so spiritual, and spiritually justified—"purpose driven" to the nines.

In hopes of qualifying my life to be worthy of this dream, the first thing I did was to clean up my mouth and commit myself to a profanity-free life. Friends had long wondered how I could have ever become a pastor with such a sailor's tongue. Now was the opportunity to show them that I was a changed man who was righteous and worthy.

Next, I went to the bookstore and purchased everything I could find written by successful conservative pastors. My desire to enjoy their same ministry fame and power was enough to turn off my brain and learn to believe, say, and do all the right "Evangelical" things, even if, deep down, some made little-to-no sense, contradicted themselves, or left good people cold, hurting, and condemned.

From there, I focused my attention on creating the appearance that all was deeply spiritual and holy within me. Repeating talking points and spiritually flavored insights that I had heard other renowned pastors say became a habitual practice in my ministry. If I could convince myself that I truly possessed a new state of heart and mind, then others would be convinced as well. I wrapped it all up in shiny Jesus paper and called it "faithfulness."

With a determination to win the prize of finally becoming lovable and worthy, I would not be stopped at believing that the conservative Evangelical brand of faith was the way, truth, and life. In fact, quickly emerging within me was the willingness to deny any voices inside of me that screamed their pleas for caution while giving increased freedom to the voices that would demonize those who disagree with me. If all else failed, I could always program more worship fog, get a tattoo, and start sporting some Buckle brand skinny jeans—the rest would take care of itself, so I believed.

To be sure, I couldn't breathe in enough of this intoxicating aroma—my flesh never felt more alive. Finally, the solution to all that was missing had arrived. Standing before me was the opportunity to "get real" with Jesus, heal my insecurities, render myself as being lovable, pay for my failings, silence my shame, and earn a place of importance in the Kingdom.

And so we did it, we jumped. My wife and I risked everything, and left all things Lutheran to the disapproval of many. We turned our back on the congregation I had been serving and prematurely cashed in our pension to supply us with a few months of living. At first, it was quite romantic, and my enthusiasm carried us through. There was now a pre-programmed way of life that simply required my allegiance. No more need for searching, thinking, questioning, or doubting. I do my part, God does His—blessings and favor will surely flow.

This was the person I was becoming. This was the life I believed was truly living. This was the salvation I was determined everyone needed—lest they burn in hell.

In fact, one evening, an old college friend stopped by for an anticipated visit. I was excited to see her as we hadn't been together since our college graduation. She knew me better than most and certainly was aware of the worldly side of my history. I wanted her to see the "new me" and validate the changes that I had been rehearsing and hoped to put on display. Before the clock struck the hour of her visit, I made sure my Bible was carefully positioned on the coffee table, and our other religious paraphernalia were in full view, not to mention some DC Talk playing in the background. With her ring of the door bell, I fluffed up my ego and desire to impress her as if I was running into a stadium for the big game. In my mind, if there was one thing she was going to see, it was that I'm a "sold out" Christian now, and everything about me would shine with a Jesus glistening. Our conversation started with my careful pastoral attention to every nuance. Yet, this time, there would be no telling of dirty jokes or reminiscing over stories of carnality from days gone by. In fact, there were more silence and awkward pleasantries than anything else. Unwavering in the moment, I took that as my cue to tell her about my faith in Jesus and my shiny new church ministry. I pulled out every talking point of expressed enthusiasm for God from my nifty conservative Evangelical bag. I was so excited for myself and how I was doing. In fact, I perceived her discomfort and hesitant nods of coerced affirmation to be a product of my successful witness. She even made the statement, "Wow, you're a changed person." The fact that her tone of voice in doing so was one of sheer panic only emboldened my Evangelical ego. I wasn't even sure exactly how her life had been going since our days in college, and honestly, I didn't really even care. All I had hoped for was that she could see that I was a new man with a new plan.

Interestingly enough, I never heard from her again. When that reality finally dawned upon me, I simply concluded, "Oh well, she had her chance."

As I closed the door of our visit and, ultimately, our relationship, deep down inside, I knew the real transformation of my soul was far from having taken place, but a religious one most certainly had secured its shackles.

People were now projects, Jesus was the springboard to my success, church was a platform upon which my ego could overcome my insecurities, and faith was an appearance that I hoped would convince me that I was something valuable when, deep down, I ultimately believed I was not.

This is the poison I thought was the cure.

"Because I remember, I despair. Because I remember, I have the duty to reject despair." -Elie Wiesel,(His) Nobel Prize Lecture

CHAPTER FOUR
Finding Bottom

I gave it my best, I really did. I never worked so hard in all my life—just ask my wife, Amy. Better yet, just ask the kids. I started waking up at 4 a.m. every Sunday morning to memorize my sermons, line-for-line, word-for-word—all for the maximum adoration of the congregation and the hopes of validating my life by becoming a superstar preacher. I began writing devotionals hoping they would get published. I read every ministry leadership book that money could buy. I attended the best conferences, taking copious notes from which to implement the latest church fads guaranteed to grow your congregation and grant you the ministry of your dreams.

I made myself available at any moment of any day for pastoral counseling or care. I studied the scriptures, applied every prayer formula I could find to maximize my capacity to leverage God for His blessings and favor. We didn't tithe just 10%, but 20%, often becoming the top givers In the churches we served whether we could afford to or not. I solicited accountability partners to speak truth into my life as a sure fire way to keep me on the straight and narrow. I distanced myself from all the right people and settings, just like I was prescribed. On Sundays, I was the first one at the church, and the last one to leave.

Those rare moments when I wasn't engaged in some kind of formal ministry, you can be sure I was thinking about it. We started churches on a wing and a prayer, barely having enough income to survive. We walked through devastating church splits, worship wars, members threatening my family, and countless conflicts, the marks of which will surely never go away. Years and years spent in a so-called "Christian life" and ministry, trying to convince God, the people around me, and myself, that I am valuable, lovable, acceptable, significant—worthy of God, His favor, His blessings, and His heaven.

With fierce devotion, I tried it all—praying, studying, worshipping, serving, giving—checking off every Evangelical item on the list. Being the best person I could be for Jesus was my ultimate goal—just as was expected. This was the hallmark of every sermon I preached. This was the foundation from which I counseled every parishioner. This was the drum that marked the beat of my footsteps for a solid 15 years of my ministry. This was the house I was building that I hoped would become a mansion of ministry success, fame, and adoration.

Yet, as much as I didn't want to disappoint nor give way to doubt and frustration, there increasingly came these moments where I was led to the edge of all that conservative Evangelical Christianity had poured into my life. It was there that I was compelled to take an honest look into the mirror and engage in a thorough evaluation of my long-held beliefs. In those pivotal moments of clarity, I was confronted and collided with the undeniable reality. If I'm honest, none of it was working—at least, not for me.

It was your typical day in Florida as I was sitting at the computer towards the back of a walk-in closet we had fashioned into a tiny office. There, I would write my messages, create worship pamphlets, manage our website, and oversee the in's and out's of church. All would have been fine that day, if that had been the extent of my activities. Sadly, it was in front of that same computer that pornography often had its grip upon me. No doubt, I strived endlessly to apply all the "conservative" principles for sexual purity. Yet, none of them worked, leaving me nothing left but to pretend. Beating my head on the desk with tears of shame and guilt bleeding down my face, I knew I was living a lie. Yet, even worse, no matter how hard I prayed, repented, and recommitted my life, none of it was working as much as I tried to convince myself otherwise.

If honesty was going to emerge from my heart, there could be no more denying. For all my efforts of obedience, this was a constant, repeating theme for nearly every issue of inadequacy in my life.

In fact, when I pulled back the curtains and stepped outside of my own denial and deception, a startling phenomenon appeared. Everyone was faking it just like me—not because we wanted to, but because, truth be told, as I was clearly discovering, that's the best one can do while on the religious treadmill of conservative Evangelical Christianity.

Trust me, I know that's hard to hear, but it is—reality.

All the formulas for prayer—didn't work. All the steps for overcoming sin through behavior management—didn't work. All the attempts to press harder into Jesus and lift Him higher—didn't work. All the inspired teachings on growing the garden of my spiritual fruits—didn't work. All the verses memorized, recited, declared, displayed, and prayed over—didn't work. All the increased commitments to church, cultivating my relationship with Jesus, and becoming a "promise-keeping" man of God and spiritual leader of my home—didn't work.

Not only did it not work, but it all left me exhausted, discouraged, empty, ashamed, and feeling even more distant from Jesus and the people He desires for me to love. At first, I thought, surely the problem is with me, I must be doing it wrong somehow. Yet, more and more, I wasn't so convinced. In fact, I was growing to not be convinced at all.

I'll never forget the moment, it was like no other. Face-to-face with a living and breathing human being who was desperately seeking hope and life, I sought to be the good and faithful Evangelical, taking everything they had taught me to be true and life-giving and apply it (verse-by-verse and line-by-line) into this broken, sin-labeled, religious, oppressed person sitting right in front of me.

She had been brutally condemned by nearly every person and spiritual entity in her life, and was grasping at my counsel for one last ray of hope. Yet, with every conservative Evangelical prescription and pre-packaged talking point that vomited off my lips, it all fell flat and reeked of death, leaving this beautiful person all the closer to giving up as the fading light behind her eyes was now all but snuffed out. What was "biblical" in Evangelical eyes, brought death to hers.

In a way like never before, the alarms went off inside of me, "Something is seriously wrong, this is not what I signed up for." This whole, "hate-the-sin, love-the-sinner" crap was showing itself to be nothing like Jesus. Broken people didn't cringe at His presence and leave defeated; instead, they clung to His every being and walked away with affirmation, freedom, and unstoppable courage.

The cat was out of the bag, and I could no longer deny it—the more conservative an Evangelical I became, the less I portrayed Jesus.

In fact, all that time, years and years, I was suffocating, when I thought I was breathing Life—thinking I was so close to Jesus, yet being so far away from His heart.

All that time, I thought I was helping people when, in fact, I was imprisoning them—declaring a mixed Evangelical gospel of conditional love that is, in fact, no Gospel at all. [1] All, while sentencing countless God-adorned people to a fear-driven, empty life of sin-management, God-appeasement, and people-judging.

All that time, I thought I was being a faithful servant when, in reality, I had become a monster—a sexist, racist, homophobic, bigoted, ignorant,

---

[1] Galatians 1:6-7

selfish, judgmental, legalistic, hypocritical, two-headed, and heart-divided monster. Without a flinch or a blink of an eye, I could heartlessly condemn people to a Dante-inspired hell of Evangelical imagination and poison their hungry, hurting hearts with guilt, shame, fear, and condemnation, all while deceiving them to believe its source was no less than the throne of God.

All that time, I thought I was equipping people when, in fact, I was using them. Call it "vision," "ministry dreams," "reaching the world for Christ," or whatever label helps you sleep at night—but, the truth is, so much of modern Christianity has simply become the franchising of ministry egos.

All that time, I thought the Bible was a kind of convenient, inerrant weapon, best used against the self-declared enemies of Jesus and for the defense of a truth that only conservative Evangelicalism possessed, when, in fact, it's actually a perfectly human set of writings best used to inspire all people to progressively encounter Him who is Love and defend His graciousness.

All that time, I thought I knew love and how to give it, when, in truth, I knew nothing of it—receiving it, living it, sharing it. I thought loving people required doing so with careful restraint for fear you might extend too much grace and affirmation, or worst of all, catch their disease. Constantly pumping the brakes with people by restricting my love and qualifying His, was indeed an unpleasant endeavor that never felt settled in my spirit. Yet, for so long, I believed that was the full extent for which God loved me—all at a safe distance, riddled with fine print.

All that time, I thought I was being the picture-perfect father and husband, but, in reality, I was so consumed by a spiritual quest in which enough was never enough, that though I may have been there physically for my family, in so many other ways, I wasn't there at all.

Leatherbound **Terrorism**

So much time wasted, relationships scorched, walls erected, people written off, unnecessary family tension and division created, opportunities missed, life that could have been enjoyed, unconditional love that could have been given, freedom that could have been embraced, lives that could have been set free by Grace, and all I had to show for it was the ever-growing, painful faith conclusion that I would never measure up, I was a failure, Jesus surely hated me, everything that mattered was slipping through my fingers, and the god of Evangelicalism was probably not only okay with it, but holy and just in allowing it, and, perhaps, even authoring it.

I know this isn't going to be easy to receive—my heart surely doesn't desire to cause hurt. But, whether you're in ministry or not, this is what you do—this is the kind of hell you live and give, in some shape or form, when your faith concludes, "God loves you... but." As unpleasant as it may be to connect the dots and gaze around the corner, there can be no more hiding of the Wizard behind the curtain. This is the performance-driven, endless, restless, futile plight of your soul when the anchor of your faith clings to the diabolical slogan made famous by conservative Evangelical Christianity, "God does His part, but you have to do yours... or else."

In fact, find me a person who subscribes to conservative Evangelicalism in whole or part, and there you will have found a beautiful soul who, chances are, is tragically sleepwalking this same kind of daily, deceived, pretending, performance-driven hell while actually believing it's heaven. I know this to be true, because it was me.

At the end of day, the conservative Evangelical elixir was wearing off as the grass was clearly no greener on the other side. Becoming a conservative Evangelical was, in fact, an outright scheme, not a dream. In fact, the very rules, forever-changing playing field, and conditions that were impossible to fulfill within my family system, were even more daunting and hopeless within the faith system of conservative

Evangelicalism. Every move towards a more conservative faith and church philosophy ultimately moved me and my wife further from the heart of Jesus, spiritual integrity, and true ministry health and success. The ministry challenges didn't go away or even subside, in fact, they only got worse. I didn't become a more loving person and pastor, I became a more selfish, judgmental, and pretentious one. My personal, spiritual, and family life wasn't better; it was just more fake, contrived, and narcissistic. The conservative spiritual and ministry path that I thought would lead to heaven, left me imprisoned to a ministry and life that increasingly felt more like hell. I tried harder and harder, convinced that I just wasn't doing it right, or my heart just wasn't "sold out" enough. Yet, with every unsuccessful push to crack the conservative Evangelical code and tip the scales, deep down inside, I felt shackled in my capacity to overcome and with no hope to ever becoming free.

Fourteen years into my ministry, it seemed like everything I touched eventually blew apart. The Evangelical dream of successful ministry always seemed to elude me—a never ending treadmill of emotionally and financially sacrificing my family at the altar of becoming and accomplishing "big" things for Jesus.

Then, all of a sudden, everything came to a boiling point, a complete breakdown.

A few years earlier, my horrible skin problems with eczema reemerged, worse than ever before, lighting my insecurities on fire and burning so much of my life to the ground. I didn't want to be seen by anyone, scratching myself to the point of bleeding. The allergic mania inflaming my entire body kept me from sleeping but only a few minutes at a time during the night. Mounds of flakey skin accumulated on the carpet below our headboard from where I itched my scalp raw. Every day was a severe struggle of physical, emotional, and spiritual torment. In fact, one of the treatments (largely unsuccessful) eventually left me half blind in one eye. The onset of these physical challenges coupled with years of failing ministry (no matter how hard I tried, and how much we sacrificed), left me with the deep levels of clinical anxiety and depression—a darkness I had never experienced before, drenched with coats of unwashable, emotional tar penetrating deep into the soul. I was a mess of worry, frustration, uncertainty, and unmanageable fear.

In light of this horrific crisis before me, everything I had been taught within my Evangelical indoctrination pushed me to conclude one simple conclusion: something was seriously wrong with me. Not only was I a failure to my father, a failure to the Father, but, now, a failure as a spiritual father, biological father, and husband. Surely, God, in His holy displeasure and wrath, was disciplining me and, even authoring, these calamities in my life. Therefore, somehow, in all my pursuits to be the faithful Evangelical, I had failed to unlock the God-code that leads to blessings, success, and prosperity, but, instead, had apparently adopted attitudes and behaviors that left God with no other choice but to press me under His thumb, that I might conform to certain aspects of His will that I had apparently missed. Only my repentance and increased obedience could reposition me under the narrow waterfall of his approval and favor. For surely, a God of conditions, requirements, and an unpredictable temper, had not moved; it was I that had strayed--and for that, there is always a price, so I learned. Once again, as it was with my father on earth, I concluded it must also be true with my Father in heaven--I wasn't good enough, despite my best efforts to surgically color inside all the Evangelical lines.

I wasn't expecting the moment to ever come. It was a scene that was far from ever being scripted in the narrative I imagined for my life. No one plans for this, but there I was, a husband, pastor, and father of two, kneeling at the side of our bed, gazing over the edge of my life, prepared and ready to jump. Shaking, sweating, emotionally raw, with a sense of doom and loneliness that had long been eating me alive.

I have never been one to give up or suffer from a lack of courage, but enough was enough.

The kids were downstairs when I heard Amy enter into our bedroom as I knelt on the floor in sheer anguish and terror. My entire being was covered with a grip of darkness that seemed to swallow me whole. This was it, the moment of no return. I told Amy, with all seriousness of intent, to divorce me, take the kids, and find a new husband and father. Their lives would be so much better. With all my health problems and a clear incapability of being successful, they deserved so much more. I pleaded and begged with Amy to be released from holding back the people I loved the most. Every moment of every day, I was a disappointment to myself, a perceived burden to others, and a barrier to the life my family deserved. Tears began to run down her eyes as her face flushed bright red. She could tell I was at the end of the end.

I'm not sure of the details of what happened next, but, somehow, my eyes closed, and an image of Jesus conquered all my senses. It was more than a visual, but a colliding, that overtook my entire being. He embraced me with His arms wrapping around my everything. I punched, cursed, yelled, denied, rebuked, condemned, putting all my strength into my fists. Yet, for all my retaliation, His grip around my life would not budge. The more I resisted and rebelled, the more resolved His hold held with incalculable divine strength. Minute, after minute, after minute. He would not let me go. He would not let me go. He would not let me go.

Incapable of breaking the determined embrace of God, my breathing settled, my soul untightened—I was exhausted. The next thing I knew, Amy was kneeling next to me with her hand grazing my sweating forehead as if I had just given birth, and a cosmic battle was finally over. For the first time in my adult life, I encountered Grace--unconditional, irrevocable, unremovable, pure, undiluted Grace. It wasn't a theology, philosophy, or new way of thinking; it was a person—Jesus. So much of what I thought and was taught was true of God, actually wasn't. He wasn't angry, condemning, judging, scorekeeping, disappointed, nor dismayed. He didn't care about anything else but loving me—nothing. There was no follow up, no fine print, no bait and switch, no add-ons nor requirements. Love was "It", the whole thing, from beginning to end—not my love for Him, but His love for me. That's all there was, that's all that was needed. Everything that enjoyed endless success at suffocating the life out of me was found to be a diabolical figment of my conservative Evangelical imagination. God was nothing like my father, and certainly nothing like the god of Evangelical Christianity. From the hospital room of my childhood to bedroom of my adulthood, my fish-named-Jesus was true. Not just true, but with me all the while.

For sure, it didn't happen overnight, but in a way and at a depth like never before, I tasted and saw that God was indeed good, really good, better than I ever imagined, far beyond the capacity of my Evangelical mind to conceive. I didn't have to rationalize Him, overlook a conservative Evangelically imposed case of divine schizophrenia placed upon Him, nor prop Him up with talking points that dance around people's doubts. He was truly good, through and through, and needed none of my conservative Evangelical snake oil to do His bidding. And best of all, now the goodness that is me, that has always been good, whole, and pure—a goodness that had long been denied and imprisoned, was suddenly given freedom to live. I was alive for the first time, breathing for the first time, loving for the first time, and allowing myself to be loved for the first time. Salvation had come—Jesus is enough, I am enough, love is enough— period, full stop. I was a man awakened by Grace in just the nick of time. Everything that truly matters began its beginning, and everything else that doesn't, started its ending.

I could no longer deny it, the revelation of my life was staring me in the face with the undeniable reality that the fruits of being a conservative Evangelical largely leave broken people more broken, loved people feeling less loved, and Jesus curled up in the corner crying in disgust at the judging, condemning, pretentious people we have become. More so than ever before, I knew deep within my being that there had to be something better than all of this. There was true Life to be had, I had tasted it for myself, but, sadly, it was becoming all too clear that I had to move beyond and outside of Evangelicalism to embrace it.

As much as I didn't want to believe it and spent copious hours arguing in my head in hopes of resisting it, the lipstick on the pig was all but worn off—conservative Evangelical Christianity had done far more than merely waste so much of my life, it had stolen every remnant of it that I had ever possessed and left me impotent to face it and its darkest moments.

Make no mistake, many within conservative Evangelicalism have hearts that are profoundly and undeniably good and intentions that are noble and surely inspired from the throne of God. Some of my best friends in all of the world subscribe to conservative Evangelicalism.

No, not all conservative Evangelicals are willing participants or knowingly support the dark side of their faith system. Of course, no church, group, denomination, or faith expression is perfect. There is no denying the great things that have come from their efforts.

Yet, the poison conservative Evangelicalism pimped as the cure had finally been exposed, and the evils chased out of the shadows. What had long been a journey of eroding imprisonment was now transformed into a new season of ever increasing and unending emancipation.

"Long is the way and hard, that out of Hell leads up to light."
—*John Milton, Paradise Lost*

CHAPTER FIVE
Embracing The Cure

I believe in angels, not out of some biblical theological requirement, but because I have experienced one in person. The residue of my depression was beginning to lift, but there continued to be sure moments where it reminded me that it was still thoroughly entrenched. I had encountered pure Grace for the first time, but unraveling the burial clothes that once suffocated me was not an instantaneous reality. Anxiety attacks were less frequent but still looming in the shadows. A dear friend named Anita had reached out to me during this dark winter of the soul. I called her, she called me—her capacity to be a spiritual guide was profound.

Shortly after the events in our upper bedroom, I was driving home from taking our son to elementary school. It was still a dark morning after dropping him off. I was preoccupied with looking at the car lights that drove past me. Though my right eye had been surgically corrected, I constantly worried that the glaucoma that nearly blinded me would return. If a halo appeared in the lights, there would be cause for concern. I was a man still smothered in fear.

Just then, in the middle of my worry-driven vigilance, my cell phone rang, it was Anita. We talked for a few minutes, but, then, something beyond my ability to put into words occurred. It was a moment like no other as her voice transformed into the undeniable voice of another. I wasn't hallucinating nor incapacitated from my ability to keep driving. In fact, I could still hear the same music playing on the car radio in the background. Yet clearly, it was no longer Anita on the phone, but a voice from the heavens. I'll never forget the powerful simplicity and crystal clarity of her words. "Chris, don't be afraid, you are perfectly loved, whole, and pure. Jesus lives in you, His Light is your light. Always has been, always will."

These words were filled with a divine freshness and weight I can't explain. I didn't fully understand their meaning nor significance just yet. Instead, they dropped a time-released Grace bomb that would soon send shockwaves, long sustaining the transformation of my entire being.

After all these years, having been seduced by a faith system that brought a living hell into every area of my life, I had tasted and seen that the conservative Evangelicalism that I had vigorously consumed was showing itself to be the true enemy. It's hard to argue with results, and the results were clear for me and my family. Conservative Evangelicalism had done far greater harm than good within me, and through me.

Now, deep within my heart as I gazed at the arising sun emerging from the horizon ahead of me, I knew there had to be a better way. A way devoid of religiosity and pretending. A way removed from hopeless performance-driven God appeasement. A way where guilt and shame are exchanged for freedom and assurance. A way where all is well, and all are well. A way where Love not only wins, but entirely removes the battle within. Thankfully, it was that angel who set this very way into motion inside of my lifeless life.

She spoke of the God who my religious mind was taught to believe was too good to be true and dangerous to consider.She spoke with a voice that swiftly usurped every religious Evangelical firewall within me.

She spoke of a God I soon discovered had embedded His Light, the faith of Christ, within me—every human an equal recipient.[2] All this time, I was feverishly pursuing something God had already granted me. This is a pivotal and powerful truth, so don't rush these words and miss it.

---

[2] John 1:4,9

In fact, here's the kicker, the revelation that begins all revelation—we all possess the faith of Jesus, a faith that fully knows and trusts the true essence and heart of the Father. He believes in us, He believes for us, and He believes with us. As it was and ever shall be from the beginning—all that is eternity. The Gospel is more than a message, it's a Person (Jesus) who has been inside of us all along, there never has been a time when He was not.[3] Everything He has, believes, and knows of the Father, we have radiating within us, beaming from within to break forth our awakening.

Yet, darkness always seeks a way to condemn and imprison the Light our soul has always possessed in hopes we never awaken to it. Soon, it becomes demonized, silenced, and even unrecognizable within us—many of us walking around unaware of the faith of Christ, His Light within us. Tragically, it all becomes so religiously deformed, twisted, covered over, trampled, and Christianized inside of us.

To be sure, if there is a Satan and He could contrive the most sinister scheme in human history to hide the true essence of God, His Light within us, and His true affections for us, in my experience, it would be conservative Evangelical Christianity for sure. For nothing eclipsed God's heart and His presence in my life so thoroughly, nearly to the point of suicide. This, is the ultimate desire of evil—pimp the poison as the cure.

In fact, Adam and Eve embraced the Light, saw themselves as Light, and gave it all a cherished harbor within. In their faith understanding, God, themselves, and all of life was a beautiful Garden—forever whole, pure, free, and alive. The faith of Christ within them had become their faith within them—a perfect communion. Yet, in a moment of question, they bit the evil lie that the Light they held to be Truth was actually darkness—needing correction, deserving of condemnation, and requiring redemption from an angry God. In their minds, all of the sudden, God became untrustworthy, Love became conditional, we became condemnable, and

---

[3] Cf. John 1:1-5; Colossians 1:15-20; 1 Corinthians 15:28

the Garden became a hopeless game of God-fearing, God-chasing appeasement. [4]

Religion is always the result of the Light becoming something to us that God isn't, we aren't, and God never had in mind. Sadly, conservative Evangelical Christianity is consummate at twisting and presenting the cure as the poison, and the poison as the cure. That's why the very Gospel of Grace that will be unfolded to you in the sentences ahead is met with such fierce objection by many conservative Christians and beyond, and, perhaps in your reading, will confront your soul and trigger your resistance, too. For when the heart of God collides with the heart of a religiously polluted humanity, what other outcome should truly be expected?

Enter Grace

As painful as the fruits of conservative Evangelical Christianity can be to bear, there is something diabolically seductive about being asleep to its evil. Deep down, I knew my family of origin was a system of lies, deception, conditions, abuse, and control, but it was the home that I learned to call home, even in its hell. For in a sense, the cross is the easier part. It takes little effort to hang suffering in wait of death, but the resurrection, the awakening to new life, is where true courage begins.

The regret of having been wrong, having lived a lie, having wasted so much time can become enough gravity to hold us captive to our denial. The last thing I wanted to believe was that my family of origin was really not a family at all, and that I was duped not just by their evil system, but a second time by the conservative Evangelical system of faith that, in essence, was just like them. I may not have chosen my family of origin, but I did choose my system of faith. How could I have been so stupid, and so easily misled by both? There was a brainwashing for sure that had

---

[4] Genesis 3

been going on for generations, and, I now fear, is deceiving the masses and spinning us into new levels of evil through its faith system of shame, guilt, fear, privilege, conditions, control, condemnation, and outright misrepresentation of God and His Gospel of peace. [5]At some point or another, we either break the cycle or we become it until we do.

Resurrection feels like death to the religious, and it surely felt like death to the religious parts that still had life within me. The very Grace that had just saved me and my family from a path of religious destruction was the very Grace I found still meeting pockets of resistance within me. Yet, despite the fears and doubts that hoped to keep me gasping for air, once again, Grace kept showing up on the television screen of my life. With every moment I wanted to return to breathing on my own, Grace showed me I wasn't breathing at all. Everytime the religious hospital that welcomed and profited from my desperation and vulnerability began to seem like a good place for a homecoming, Grace showed me the hell it was requiring and making of me. Everytime the banshees of conservative Evangelicalism still haunting in my head called me back into their dungeons, Grace reminded me of their destruction that is always forthcoming. Everytime I wondered if sleeping my life away upon the comfortably numb beds of conservative Evangelicalism would be better, Grace kept reviving me and pushing me out of the door, gifted with an IV bag full of hope to empower me.

With a relentlessness that never gives up, Grace is God pinging your soul in hopes of awakening you to the true Light you have always possessed and your heart has longed to believe.[6] It's the call of Jesus to be unwrapped from the burial clothes that bind your heart from embracing true Life. For religion rings true to the flesh, but Grace rings true to the soul.[7] It's the Deep calling to your depth. It's the true faith of Christ within

---

[5] Ephesians 6:15
[6] Psalm 136
[7] Galatians 3

you crying out to become your faith within you.[8] It's the moment your religious, christianized understanding is overridden by your Spirit and though you can't explain it and your mind can't chart it, you taste the Light and your heart knows it to be True, even as it shakes you to your core. It's breathing for the first time and realizing, all this time you weren't breathing at all. It's Grace releasing, rekindling, and recalibrating the caverns of your soul to what it's always known and your heart has longed to believe—all is Grace.[9]

This is the cure, the message from God you've probably never truly heard before, but your soul has always believed deep within, and your heart is desperate for you to embrace—God is Love, period. [10]

This is the awakening that saved my life, marriage, ministry, and family.

This is the revelation that frustrates every religious cell in our souls as it shoots its spiritual antibiotic into the puss-ladened core of the conservative Evangelical infection that would devour us.

Hear me, and hear me well. Whatever sense of condemnation, shame, disappointment, or lack you have towards yourself (or others), it does not come from God—it can't. Run from any message that puts any conditions, any hell, or any distance between you and Him. Contrary to what is largely taught throughout American Christianity, all of these are constructs of religious projection and sure poison to the soul.

Grace awakens our perceptions to the true nature of God and His all-inclusive affection for us. The purpose of Christ is not simply that we believe in Him, but that we believe in God like Him—His faith within us becomes our faith within us.[11] For Jesus knows no other nature, aspect,

---

[8] Galatians 2:16
[9] Ephesians 2:8
[10] 1 John 4:8
[11] Galatians 2:20; Philippians 3:9

or trait of God other than pure, unconditional Love. His sinless life before God is our sinless life before God—His performance in life is our performance in life. Love is all, defines all, wins all, and conquers all—especially us. Jesus has no sense of God as being nor exuding anything but unyielding Love. Therefore, we should never entertain a thought about God or ourselves that God doesn't first have of Himself and us.

Thus, to the delight of our soul, when we finally allow ourselves to see God the way Jesus does, we discover there is no other message from God to and for our lives other than Love—no fine print, conditional clauses, trap doors, loopholes, or dropping axes. Love unhinges the tenets of the religious and reveals the evil forces behind their call to one-eyed open living, sin-managing, God-appeasing, self-improving, people-judging, and hell-fearing. Only the graceless, self-righteous, privileged, and judgmental ever feel the force of God's displeasure as Grace confronts their religious, doubting, selfish, love-drained souls. In fact, the only two places recorded In Scripture where Jesus specifically becomes angry are not at people withholding judgment or condemnation, but both exclusively at people withholding Grace.[12]

God is Love from top to bottom, beginning to end—inside and out. The expanse of God who is Love is boundless, limitless, unrestricted, and unrestrained. His actions and reactions to every molecule and movement of your life is always Love. God is pedal-to-the-metal in love with you—always has been, always will be.

This is the Grace that has always been flowing like a river in your soul, seeking to break the dams of religiosity that hold you captive and well up in you with streams of life everlasting and overflowing.

---

[12] Mark 3:4-6, Mark 10:14

"Hope is the only bee that makes honey without flowers."
—Robert Green Ingersoll

CHAPTER SIX
Learning To Breathe, Learning To Believe

The greatest enemy to an asthmatic is trying harder. When you're in the middle of an attack, everything in your flesh is telling you to breathe deeper, think more positively, subdue your emotions, and get back in control. At first, every effort feels like it's helping you and the quickest path to overcoming. Yet, the truth is, it's those very efforts to breathe that could cause you to not be able to breathe at all—life and death are in the balance. When it came to surviving asthma, learning to truly breathe saved my life.

In the same way, nothing prevents the oxygen of God's Grace from breathing real life into your soul like the conservative Evangelical faith system of trying harder, doing more, and living in perpetual fear of a god who could love you one moment, but send you to the hell the next. In conservative Evangelical Christianity, at the end of the day, it's all up to you—life and death are in the balance. At first, it feels like it's working and the sure path to overcoming. Yet, the truth is, everything conservative Evangelicalism had taught me about having faith turned out to be the very things that were keeping me from truly having it. None of it was working, all of it was suffocating. When it came to surviving the spiritual asthma that is conservative Evangelical Christianity, learning to truly believe saved my life.

His name was Rod Fleischer, he had been a part of my early ministry and development. He believed in me with a sweetness and generosity that was beautifully unique. Yet, in all my conservative Evangelical prowess to console Him in his time of suffering and death, he could see right through me. When I would come to visit him in the hospital, like any faithful Evangelical, I was sure to have all the answers and biblical verses to coincide. There were no deep mysteries that I couldn't reduce to black and white—so I believed.

On one afternoon visit that would, sadly, prove to be my last, Rod had endured a difficult night before. He knew that the medications had met their match, and his alternatives were increasingly few. I pulled up a chair beside him, waiting for a moment to interject some profound statement of faith and explanation to connect all the dots. He knew the drill, but this time politely stopped me before I could get started, turning his head to me with a question, "Chris, have you ever taken the Nestea Plunge? You know the commercial, don't you?" I answered affirmatively, "Yes, of course." He then told me how the night before He had realized that he was soon going to die and could no longer fight it. All the ramifications for his wife and teenage daughter he could no longer bear. The thoughts of missing out on their lives had been spinning him into despair. He couldn't understand it, reconcile it, nor explain God's hand in it, and was desperately tired of trying. At that moment of complete loss and emptiness, he arose in his hospital bed and put his hands in the air in complete surrender, and laid back in unexplainable assurance like the guy falling backwards into the pool taking the "Nestea plunge." After a moment of pause to make sure I was still listening, Rod then moved his head closer to me as if to look into my soul. He gently asserted, "Chris, I can tell you are a man of faith, but not yet a man of rest; there's a difference. You lack one thing which is everything, the Nestea plunge into Grace."

Theology and the Christian life are like sex, no one likes to be told they're doing it wrong. Yet, the truth was, for all my conservative Evangelical faith, I was, in fact, a man whose faith was no faith at all, but, rather, a spiritual veil to a restless empty life.

I had so much to learn, the most important and life-changing of which Rod was dying for me to receive--a simple, but profound, cosmic altering truth… to believe is to rest.

Nothing more, nothing less.

It's not to behave, it's not to become, it's not even to behold.

It's not to figure out, study it out, or even work it out.

To believe is to rest.

It was this timely remembrance of that last conversation with Rod, a conversation that had long been forgotten, that set into motion a deep rethinking of most everything I once held to be true. I was a man learning to breathe and believe for the first time. I was a life resurrecting.

In fact, with each moment that my soul was increasingly centered on Grace, the unrelenting restlessness, anxiety, and religious spirit within was increasingly subdued and rendered impotent. Piece by piece, the clothes of conservative Evangelical Christianity that buried me alive were beginning to unravel. In increasing fashion, the panic attacks diminished and my toxic religious need to punish myself (and others) with guilt, shame, religious rule-keeping, and fear was depleting. For the first time in my life I felt the presence of true faith, not because I tried harder, but because I tried less. I wasn't grasping for something more, I was awakened to what I already had. My self-talk could finally speak life as I learned to remind my soul that I am the righteousness of Christ--whole, pure, without blemish, and lacking no spiritual blessing. When I recalled the Scripture writer who spoke of God declaring, "Be holy, for I am holy," [13] the scales were now lifted from my eyes so that I could finally see that these words were a divine declaration, not of what I needed to become, but to be bravely be who I already am--holy. With these words, it was

---

[13] Cf Leviticus 11:44-45; 1 Peter 1:16

nothing less than the voice of Jesus admonishing me (and you), "Do you! You are enough, because I am enough. Rest and believe."

For the first time in my life, I was breathing—I was learning to rest, I was learning to believe.

With every step of new freedom into my awakening to Grace, mind-changing and soul-stirring questions would emerge, not only about God, but about the Christian life—beliefs I had long held to be true. What amount of sin adds up to a lifestyle of it? What amount of do-gooding adds up to faithfulness? What amount of trusting adds up to truly believing? What is a "relationship" with God, anyway? What amount of prayer, studying, fellowship, and adoration amounts to being a true worshipper? What amount of faithfulness adds up to being a genuine Christian? Tell me, who gets to decide any of this, anyway? Me? You? Which one of the over 30,000 Christian denominations that read the same Bible, but arrive at vastly different conclusions, is right?

These are the kinds of questions that collided with my religious soul and forced my honesty.

The truth I had to admit is that nobody really knows for sure, the playing field is always changing depending on which flavor of Christianity is on your tongue at any given moment. Even on our best day, our capacity to simply believe is inadequate if we're honest and humble enough before God to admit it.

In fact, with each layer of deception and denial that was peeled off of my soul, it became increasingly clear that to be a player on the conservative Evangelical team, one must first become a pretender who's skilled at faking it, especially when it comes to faith and faithfulness. For with a faith-understanding that places its success and legitimacy largely on our abilities, behavior, and capacity to believe correctly and adequately (whatever that means), we will always be people who, in truth, can do nothing more than mostly fake it.

That's exactly what I had spent most of my spiritual life doing--faking it. Pretending to have all the answers when I certainly didn't. Portraying a life of holiness and faithfulness when my real life was far from it. Spewing out all the talking points, hoping to convince myself and others they were the divine precepts we needed to adopt, even when I wasn't so convinced. Hiding my true doubts and insecurities, making sure to not let anyone in. Playing by the rules and falling in line, simply because I thought that was how to win. No wonder it all came crashing down.

Thankfully, despite what many may hold to be true, I discovered that faith is not a decision, choice, or invitational response. Instead, faith is a gift from God welling up from within.[14] It's the awakening of our heart, mind, and soul to the Jesus that has always been within us (and all humanity), and the God whose arms have always been wrapped around us.

I realize this assertion shakes a very foundational pillar of the temple of Evangelical theology, but it's critically true.

Rod was right. To believe is to rest in Grace and the illimitable goodness of God, trusting its full sufficiency for every aspect of our lives. In fact, pursuing God, chasing after God, hungering for more God, and begging God to come, bless, and even forgive, though all seemingly innocent spiritual pursuits, are actually confessions that He is not already here. They speak of our true sentiments toward God that His grace is not sufficient, His cross was impotent, and His choosing of us is somehow inadequate. For in the end, a restless, appeasing, and fearing heart before Jesus is a disbelieving heart before Jesus. With that revelation. the truth was standing right before me in the mirror that the best that conservative Evangelical Christianity could do was to make me into a poser.

---

[14] Ephesians 2:8

In fact, just ask Peter, who, even though he pledged his loyalty to Jesus and committed to love him completely, ended up denying him three times. Why? Because his best efforts, like ours, always eventually break down, and in the end are shown for what they are—filthy rags of self-righteous evil and disbelief.[15]

In contrast, Grace postures our entire being onto a foundation of rest—convinced we can never over-portray, over-trust, or over-characterize the goodness, love, sufficiency, and graciousness of God, nor can we ever believe too much in the unsurpassed power of Grace to guide, change, and enable us in all things.[16]

Believing in the unfathomable Love that is God and declaring this Love to be His singularity of heart, mind, and will, is not a sign of human weakness, faith depravity, or theological waywardness. If anything, it is our under-believing, under-ascribing, under-estimating, and under-characterizing of His Love purity that reveals the x-ray of our religiously-infected souls as in our doubts and flesh addiction, we live our lives restlessly turning outside of Jesus to find peace with God, peace with ourselves, and peace with people.

Grace Is The Gospel, Not Repentance

It was from this posture of rest that waves of divine cosmic revelation began to penetrate my soul and recalibrated my everything. The more the religious mind within me was subdued, the more the mind of Christ within me could be heard. What He revealed to me was nothing less than life-changing.

So much of what I believed to be true and life-giving was found to be much the opposite. It didn't happen overnight, but it was happening. With

---

[15] Isaiah 64:6
[16] Ephesians 3:18

72

one new breath at a time, I was learning to believe as I began to discover the power of Grace for living.

In fact, I was reminded of one particular occasion as a conservative Evangelical Pastor when, for some reason, once again, I just couldn't crack the church-growth and ministry-fame code that it seemed other pastors had somehow mastered. As I had done many times before, I crunched the spiritual numbers into my conservative Evangelical calculator in hopes of discovering the problem. The results always came back the same. There must be an area of unconfessed sin in my life eclipsing me from God's ministry blessings. In step with the precepts of conservative Evangelical grooming, I "recommitted" myself to daily time spent in focused repentance and seeking the favor of God. Sometimes, I would spend hours a day for months-on-end hoping to wrench open the hands-of-God's renewal upon my life and ministry.

Yet, as hard as I tried to push all the right buttons, nothing ever improved, and a spiritual angst gained further footing in my heart. All this "repentance," formulas for prayer, and pressing into Jesus stuff was showing itself to be a scam, especially when other pastors and Christians who clearly lived duplicit lives were enjoying ministry success beyond imagination. To be sure, I am familiar with the notion that God sends rain upon the just and unjust. In fact, it's a common talking point used by conservative Evangelicals when their spiritual prescriptions of "getting right with God" don't work.

That's why, what conservative Evangelical Christianity fears most is that we all discover, when it's all said and done, there is only one cure in life, and it's not the Bible, church, prayer warriors, retreats, accountability partners, or even repentance—it's Grace.

Grace is the only power that changes anything—especially people. For sure, it was the only power that changed me.

The good news isn't that God offers us a gift, but we must respond in order to receive it—that's the conservative Evangelical interpretation of the Gospel, and it's not good news: it's terrible news. For who knows when one truly believes, repents, and behaves well enough and properly enough for the exchange to truly occur, let alone remain. If it's up to us in any way, shape, or form, there will always be doubt, fear, and uncertainty waiting eagerly in the wings—all sure poisonous fruits of evil.

The reason why my life and ministry was tossed and toppled over by the storms raging around me wasn't because I didn't believe in a Gospel, it's because I believed in the conservative Evangelical gospel of "repentance," which is no Gospel at all.

See, the truly good news is that our unconditional, irreversible inclusion in Christ with all its benefits is the gift—there's nothing to receive, only everything to believe. When Jesus said, "It's finished," He meant it.[17] Faith is simply awakening and resting fully in this Truth—realizing it's never been about our performance, but always about His. Any "repentance" and relational aspects of Scripture must be understood, not as admonitions for our required response, but as cues to awaken to the fullness and sufficiency of Grace that is already ours, completely and irrevocably. This difference changes everything, and makes the Gospel truly good news.

Sadly, what crack cocaine is to a drug addict, "repentance" has become to conservative Evangelical Christianity. Tragically, as it was for me, in the end, all it does is leave good people wasted on the streets of conservative Evangelical spiritual depravity where nothing ever truly gets better, only worse. In fact, it wasn't until Grace detoxified my heart and believing of its repentance-driven evil religiosity that true life, ministry success, life improvement, and personal significance became realities. For Grace so humbled my pretentious, conservative Evangelical heart and demolished my spiritual pride, that I finally became postured for true

---

[17] John 19:30

success, having realized that it looks so much different through the eyes of Jesus.

I was now a man learning to repent of my repentance-driven religious life. To think that true freedom from always trying to measure up and keep God interested could actually become a reality was refreshing my soul in a way like never before.

Finally, I was learning to believe.

You Are The Relationship

With a new wind filling my sails, I then discovered how damaging the popular Evangelical idea of having a "relationship" with God was to my faith and faithfulness.

The modern Christian idea that God wants a "relationship" with us is highly misleading and, in fact, unfounded in scripture. Interestingly enough, there is not even a single mention in all the Bible of "inviting Jesus into your heart." Rather, the concept of a personal relationship with Jesus has been projected back into the Bible and onto the Gospel by our fleshly, religious desire to have some level of human control and credit with God, and even a spiritual notch on our belt that distinguishes us as above others.

A "relationship" requires the performance, maintenance, and continual contributing desire of both parties. Thus, a relationship can have varying levels of closeness and even become completely broken.

Thankfully, this is not what we have with Jesus nor what He has in mind with or for us. Instead, the Gospel proclaims our communion with God, established long before our earthly arrival and even before His.

Our union with God is of the same fabric as the Trinity. It is not a relationship, it is a singular entity based not on desire, performance, or the like, but is, in fact, a whole union. We are not in a relationship with Christ, we are actually in Christ--He is in us, we are in Him, inseparably.[18] Jesus is not a person to invite into your life or heart; He is your life and heart, irrevocably.

This is a profound awakening, revealed by Grace and manifested by Jesus. There is no "relationship" with Jesus, God, or the Holy Spirit to be had, for we ARE the relationship—different, but equally connected. Thus, in full union and communion.

Therefore, the Gospel doesn't become real the moment one invites Jesus into their heart, it becomes real the moment they realize He has been there all along.

This revelation changed my life and dismantled so much of my religious believing and being. It was a key that unlocked so many prisons that conservative Evangelicalism had constructed within me.

The voice on the television in the hospital, the fish named Jesus of my childhood--it's true, all of it. That He has been with me and within me all along, unconditionally and inseparably, convinced my heart He will never leave. And because He will never leave, I am finally free to live. Finally free to breathe and believe--without fear or restriction.

To think that, all along, what I truly had with God was nothing less than an effortless, fail-proof, inseparable, divine communion was opening my eyes to a joy that was immeasurable, but also to a regret for all the time wasted striving to have and keep a "relationship" that never existed.

Finally, I was learning to believe.

---

[18] Galatians 3:26-28

Jesus Equalizes Everyone

From there, I soon discovered, there was much more to this newfound rest and power than merely the freedom it was bringing to me. Its emancipation and impact can be seen upon nothing less than all of humanity.

For Grace is the great equalizer—none are better, only different.[19] All are loved, all are affirmed, and all are valued and equal in capacity—Jesus makes it so. Equality isn't just an important social value; it's nothing less than what the Gospel looks like when manifested upon the earth.

Sadly, nearly everything about the conservative Evangelical creed speaks of and fosters privilege, the opposite of His Kingdom—"we" are the saved, "you" are the lost; we are the faithful, you are the heathen; we are the blessed, you are the condemned; we are the friends of God, you are the enemy; we are the sole possessors of Biblical understanding and righteous interpretation, you are the sure heretics; we are the faith upon which this nation was founded, you are the people that need to be converted and conquered.

It wasn't until I experienced the humbling joy of seeing myself as completely equal with all humanity and valuing everyone all the same (as does Jesus) that I truly understood that Grace had fully awakened in my heart.

For it's not likely to be found written in the church bulletin or the carefully crafted mission statement of your local conservative Evangelical Church, but with white-painted churches, steepled with white crosses as far as the eye can see, Sunday mornings across America can be some of the most segregated hours of the week, and a screaming indictment to the true fruits being grown on the vine of significant segments of conservative

---

[19] Cf Luke 15:3-7; Matthew 18:12-14

77

Evangelical Christianity—division, supremacy, sexism, racism, and classism, all of which are the poison, not the cure.

To think that what I once cherished most about Christianity was the separateness, privilege, and platform of distinction I thought it brought to me, only to realize the Gospel comes to bring the opposite—inclusivity, equality, and equal affirmation of all. This revelation both pulverized my religious arrogance and liberated my spirit with a new outlook upon myself and all of life.

Finally, I was learning to believe.

Condemnation And Conditions Are Messages Of The Devil

In fact, the Spirit wouldn't stop with simply revealing the deplorable nature of inequality, but would lead me to understand the sinister evil of all forms of condemnation and conditions.

For how can we condemn or constrain anyone with conditions when Jesus lives in all, and loves and affirms all unconditionally?

Make no mistake, Jesus didn't die to riddle your life (or any other) with condemnation in any form. Jesus doesn't love you to fill your heart with conditions. Jesus didn't create heaven to lose you to the possibility of hell. For any message that declares condemnation from God or places conditions to love, falls drastically short of reflecting God and understanding Him who is Love.

Even as I write, I truly wish I could give it to you, but I can only share what I know to be true and hope it breaks through. There is neither condemnation nor conditions in Christ.[20] And here's the kicker, all are in

---

[20] Romans 8:1

Christ from the very beginning.[21] This is perhaps the one true revelation that paddle-shocked my broken heart the most with the power to leap at His.

Find me a person who struggles with pornography, gossip, gluttony, greed, or any form of all the other sins, and there you will have found a person who suffers not from a performance problem, but from a condemned heart. For the only card Satan can play in your life is the card of condemnation, it's the root of all that goes wrong within us.

That's why Jesus didn't tell the woman caught in adultery by the conservative Evangelicals of her day to come under one of their "accountability partners" and sign up for one of their Adultery 101 classes, but, rather, drew a message in the sand that sent those religious conservatives packing. I suspect he wrote the one and only word that He knew for sure would repel them and heal her condemned heart at the same time, "Grace." And, then, He simply whispered the Gospel in six words right into her ear, "There is nothing wrong with you. There's no one left to condemn you, and neither do I. Sin, no longer need master you."

Sadly, the most popular talking points being spouted by conservative Evangelical Christianity aren't messages of life-freeing Grace. Rather, topping the list are talking points like, "God loves you... but," "Turn or burn," and "Hate the sin, love the sinner." All, sure messages of conditions and condemnation. For in God's eyes, there is no such thing as loving the "sinner," because He doesn't see anyone in that way nor make that label even a true possibility. Instead, He calls them "friend," "saint," "child," "blessed," "righteous" and "heirs" in the Kingdom, seeing all people included in Himself as Himself, unconditionally.

To think that I no longer had to prequalify people for love (including myself) and spiritual police the world with conditions and condemnation,

---

[21] John 1:1-5

79

brought an emancipation to my heart that was freeing me from the slavery of conservative Evangelical religiosity.

Finally, I was learning to believe.

No, God Doesn't Send Tragedy

And perhaps most healing of all, I discovered the true heart of God and His affections for me and all of humanity.

I discovered that God was not the author of my misfortune, misery, or adversity. He wasn't the terrible parent whose best idea for bringing about transformation is to slice and dice into people's lives with the sword of punishment and tragedy.

With His arms wrapped in an unbreakable seal around my very being, one thing was for sure on the floor in our upper bedroom as He held me, His heart was only filled with unrestrained affirmation and affection for me. He would rather die and put an end to all reality than to see me suffer for any reason, that's how tight His squeeze is.

All the adversity, pain, and horror I had experienced wasn't about revenge, retaliation, punishment, or some twisted form of divine discipline. This was about the fruits of conservative Evangelicalism being revealed for what they truly are—evil.

I now imagine that nothing (not even sin) frustrates God more than when people misrepresent His heart and ways—the copious amounts of time He must spend face-palming at every negative dot we connect to Him.[22]

In fact, so much of conservative Evangelical Christianity is rooted and motivated by what it stands against and the imperialistic separateness it

---

[22] Matthew 7:21-23

desires to have from and over the rest of the world. Therefore, nothing is perhaps more intoxicating to the conservative Evangelical heart than connecting God to the bad things that are happening in the lives of those with whom they disagree or despise.

To be sure, it's a telling gaze into the true essence of one's faith when their default setting for filling in the blanks of God's movement in the lives of people is always bent towards concluding that a vengeful god of retribution and punishment must surely be working behind the scenes. When a tragedy brings devastation, God is quickly deemed to be the angry, white-bearded captain at the helm, steering a course of divine retribution. When a child dies from cancer, God is quickly suspected as working directly and intentionally to teach a lesson or bring about some kind of better future that could not have been rendered without this divine intervention—as twisted and evil as that would surely be.

Thankfully, I realized it was high time for me to grow past anchoring my faith to the limited revelation of biblical writers who personified God as the author of atrocious events and occurrences in which He surely had no part or influence. In fact, we Christians would do well to stop echoing the popular, pre-packaged message of modern Christianity that flippantly declares, "God Is In control." This oversimplified sentiment, though perhaps well intentioned, falls desperately flat in the heart and mind of good-thinking people who refuse to believe in a god who would author evil. In fact, God surely paces the halls of heaven in dire disgust with every characterization and conclusion that connects His fingers with the misfortunes of others.

With all of this revelation pouring into my soul, as hard as it was to admit, Grace held up a mirror to my depths, only to reveal, it was I who desired to be in control, not God.

It was the religious spirit within me that gave birth to such distorted images of the Father and His ways, not God.

It was I who would wield such destruction in the lives of those I deemed to be wayward while hoping to spiritually justify it all, not God.

For God is the author of freedom, not the orchestrator pulling the strings of disaster.

He is Love, not the leader of tragedy.

He is Grace, not the bestower of punishment.

In fact, here's a tip for the journey. If you find that God always seems to be the enemy of your enemies and working calamity into the lives of the very same people your faith stands against, chances are, you have raped Jesus into a missile of your own religious targeting system. So much so, that when tragedy and hardship come to those you believe to be in violation of God's will, He is quickly deemed as being just, holy, and a clear ally working directly on behalf of your faith. Yet, when difficulty and disaster come to your doorstep or those aligned with your creeds, God is suddenly personified as being mysterious and beyond one's capacity to fully understand. These convenient conclusions smell of a person desiring to spiritually justify hate and harm and use God to manipulate and control others.

No, God doesn't send tragedy.

Instead, He sent His Son to save us all from believing He ever would.[23]

No, condemnation and conditions are not messages from God.

Instead, His Grace is sufficient and His love endures forever.[24]

---

[23] John 3:17
[24] 2 Corinthians 12:9; Psalm 136; 1 Chronicles 16:34

No, separatism, elitism, privilege, discrimination, and pretentiousness are not products of the Gospel.

Instead, true equality and human servanthood are what the Gospel looks like when it flowers into full fruition.

No, inviting Jesus into your heart, saying the right prayer, and following the rules doesn't bring about nor sustain our connection with God.

Instead, all are in Christ irrevocably and inseparably from the foundation of eternity.

No, repentance is not the Gospel.

Instead, all is Grace.

Indeed, I was a man learning to breathe, I was a man learning to truly believe for the first time.

"Sometimes the Bible in the hand of one man is worse than a whisky bottle in the hand of (another)... There are just some kind of men who - who're so busy worrying about the next world they've never learned to live in this one, and you can look down the street and see the results." — *Harper Lee, To Kill a Mockingbird*

CHAPTER SEVEN
Leatherbound **Terrorism**

For 40 years, I believed that my parents fundamentally loved me. Sure, we had our disagreements and difficult moments. However, particularly into my adulthood, I never thought that their overall relationship with me as their child was in jeopardy. Despite all the family tensions and question marks raised by my abuse, I never would have considered these conclusions to be misguided and worthy of insecurity. If there was one thing that seemed infallible and unshakeable in my life, it was the overall certainty that my parents' acceptance of me as their own child would always endure. Perhaps it was all wishful thinking or a slow, steady stream of denial trickling deep within me, but up until my father died and, later, my mother, the thought of being orphaned by my parents never entered onto my radar screen.

I wish It were different, but I can't find much good to speak about my biological sister. Where she had every opportunity to break the vicious cycle of our toxic family system of conditional love, greed, deception, selfishness, abuse, and evil, she has sadly made a life of excelling at it and extending its darkness. So much so, that she even lured our fragile and vulnerable mother into her black web of seduction. Having just lost her husband (my father) and suffering from previous strokes, my aging mother displayed an emotional and physical illness that showed itself to be an opportunity for exploitation my sister simply couldn't resist.

I'm not sure how it was all orchestrated since it was done in secret over a period of several years, but I'll never forget the results. Shortly after my mother passed away, I knew I had responsibilities with regard to her and my father's will. It took some time, but I finally located all the documents that had long been filed away. As much as I disliked having to communicate with my sister, I knew my responsibility to my parents' wishes required it. After reaching out to her to begin the process, there was no reply. I even offered for us to communicate between our lawyers; she refused. A few days later, I received several large envelopes from her lawyer. I'm not a person who is easily shocked, and it takes a lot for me to lose my breath, but what I was about to read nearly sucked the life out of my lungs in a way that hadn't occurred for years. In those envelopes were documents that revealed that my mom and sister, on their own, had completely changed the original will and added expressed words that I was no longer considered a child of the family. In concert with my father's earlier declaration from my youth, "He's no son of mine," my mother now joined in the chorus to add her final conclusion and statement, "He's no son of mine either."

There are no words to express what's it like to learn that something so important and foundational, that you held to be so true, certain, and trustworthy was in fact much to the contrary. A collapse in reality of this magnitude is soul shaking. There's nothing like the bitter cold awareness that you have been deceived, not just for a moment, but for nearly a lifetime. One truth, chased out of shadows, rendered the complete downfall of the integrity of my entire family system. In every way but biological, I was never truly their child. The family secret was no longer a secret anymore. In fact, my family had never been my family at all.

Sometimes in life, we don't realize the things silently deceiving us—false beliefs we have long held to be true, misplaced values we have long embraced as being invaluable. As humans, we can be so attracted to the path of least resistance that we become willing to reject the kind of information that would free us from our prisons. To think that we could be wrong, misled, or have wasted our lives on things found to be untrue or uncertain is a daunting proposition of regret we'd just as soon put to death, even if it means resigning ourselves to a life holding fast to the lies.

Take it from me, no one wants to learn that their family system is indeed false and riddled with lies to the point of being, in actuality, no family at all. In the same way, I suspect no one wants to learn that their faith system is concealing a family secret that, when revealed, sends its integrity and entire legitimacy crashing to the ground. Yet, sadly, this is exactly what I ultimately discovered about the faith system of conservative Evangelical Christianity.

Within conservative Evangelicalism, there is a lie so foundational to its existence that its discovery collapses the entire faith system to the ground. In fact, it reveals nothing less than the true diabolical nature of conservative Evangelicalism and its overriding central desire for power and control. Like the evil Death Star of the Empire, conservative Evangelicalism has a fatal design flaw of vulnerability that when revealed, explodes its faith system into smithereens. Its ability to conquer the universe, and war its imperialism across the planet, is thoroughly dismantled. No longer will its weapon of terrorism work to conform, control, and conquer the world into their ideology. That's why its secrecy, protection, denial, and cover up is so important. For if you pull back the curtain and discover the Wizard is a hoax, fear can no longer have its power. The gates will be unlocked, and the prisoners will be set free as the Evangelical Empire is revealed of its sorcery.

Sadly, power, control, and privilege are highly seductive, and the greatest wielder of deception and keeper of lies. And for the Christian, nothing enables the fruition of this pursuit and addiction more fully than declaring the infallibility of the Bible and the exclusive, divine authority of one's interpretation of it. When you believe and declare that God has given you His words perfectly and your understanding of them is uniquely authoritative and sanctioned by God, there is no limit to what can be spiritually rationalized. This intoxicating, self-declaration of divine power and anointing walls itself off from all challenges of criticism and accountability by simply demanding, "This is what the Bible says," and those who disagree do so because they are not spiritual enough to receive it. What a perfect concoction for the unlimited birth of evil. For biblical infallibility and exclusive interpretive authority pours a kind of spiritual gasoline on the hell-lit fires of power, greed, violence, hate, control, and privilege with an intoxication and propensity for evil that is unprecedented.

In fact, if you hold to the conservative Evangelical beliefs I once did, you are likely determined that outside of your conservative Evangelical way of thinking and believing, there is essentially no other way, no other truth, and no other life. Mainly, this is because you have been told and believe that your faith is founded on the Scriptures (which to you is the perfect Word of God), and your interpretation uniquely reflects its "clear teachings." As noble, Godly, and innocent as that resolve may seem, it is actually the very same evil way of framing one's faith that has become the breakfast from which good-hearted Christians become those who would weaponize the Scriptures in hopes of defending and spiritualizing their own depravity, desire for power, lust for privilege, and thirst for control as they seek to combat and conquer a "lost" world.

For me, it didn't all happen at once; the erosion was much more subtle.

Compared to the person I am becoming now, it's hard to believe I was once the husband, father, and pastor who would callously use Scripture in ways that would hurt and harm others, even the ones I loved the most. Soon, the Bible served as a way to dehumanize people (even my own family) and create a spiritual justification for my lack of apathy and compassion, and an increased willingness to condemn, punish, and harm. Sadly, I didn't even realize the monster I had become. It all seemed so right and so spiritual. Better yet, I felt so powerful, sure, and special. When you take the Bible literally, twist it carefully, and quote it like a machine gun spraying into a crowd, what could possibly go wrong? I can't stress enough how numb I was to the seduction of it all. In my mind, I was simply defending and asserting the faith I believed was infallibly true through the Bible that infallibly told me so. To me, people were going to hell, further destroying their lives, and remaining enemies of God unless they came into my exact system of faith, thinking, and behaving. I probably wouldn't have put it into these same words back then, but I ultimately believed that God was my commander, the Bible was a kind of divinely commissioned weapon, the world was a battlefield, and my purpose was to be a good soldier. Sadly, I didn't realize that with that brand of believing in charge of my soul, no one was safe—especially Jesus.

Certainly not the young woman who came to my church office hoping simply to receive some basic peace and comfort for her life. She had recently had an abortion, having been raped at a party. I listened for a few minutes to fulfill my pastoral duties, all the while locking and loading the conservative Evangelical talking points in my head, ready to fire. It was almost as if, no matter what she said, I had already concluded the situation was somehow her fault and a product of her embracing sin in her life. After she finished telling her story, I shared a brief word of understanding to soften the blow, then quickly moved to the Scriptures to admonish her about the "biblical" consequences of murder and being sexually loose in attitude or appearance. With one final crescendo, I felt it highly important to make it clear that regardless of how it may or may not have happened, her repentance was required, but would likely never heal her shame, and rightly so. The countenance in her eyes was one I'll never forget as her face was filled with shock, horror, and hopelessness. I proudly thought I had done my job, tragically unaware that I had accomplished Satan's. Sadly, what she experienced in those moments of vulnerability and desperate need, countless others would have to endure over the span of my ministry.

Leatherbound **Terrorism**

This is the kind of callous, brainwashed person I had become who hesitated not in committing countless acts of leatherbound terrorism, deserving of nothing less than the status of a vicious war criminal.

For some, even as they watch their marriage erode, their children suffer the rejection and abandonment of their condemnation, their faith-performance fall short, their hypocrisy grow, and their hate and intolerance overtake them, nothing will loosen the grip they have upon their conservative faith understanding, especially with regard to the Scriptures. Maybe for you, as you continue to read, your fingers are twitching, your soul is fidgeting, and your mind is rushing ahead to the bullets you'll fire in response to this chapter. Perhaps, you have it all lined up and justified in your mind and heart, along with the biblical passages and interpretations to build your defense. In your mind, nothing is worthy, nor will ever be successful at questioning your determination to hold fast to your conservative Evangelical grasp on the Bible.

Yet perhaps as admirable as your tenacity may be, little do you know, conservative Christianity is killing you—a death that is largely orchestrated by a toxic view and relationship with the Scriptures. Maybe you would do well to ask your spouse—or even better, to question your children. Ask your enemies, those you deem to be sinning, or those with whom you disagree. Ask the females, the minorities, the lesbian, gay, bi-sexual, or transgender people among you, or perhaps just ask the less fortunate. For if they are honest and objective, they will tell you the dark, diabolical tale of what conservative Christianity has truly done through the leatherbound terrorism many have embraced.

But, if not them, maybe, just maybe, your conscience has been speaking, crying out to be heard. Deep down, you sense something isn't quite adding up; there are pieces all together missing. You quickly subdue the tensions in your soul, the questions that tremble below, and cue the conservative Evangelical talking points and "biblical" rationalizations.

Hear my heart plead with yours to give way to honesty and awaken to the truth that is so desperately trying to set you free—conservative Evangelical Christianity is killing you (and not just you) with its weaponizing of the Scriptures.

With countless translations and different interpretations of the Bible—from Calvinism to Arminianism, from Universalism to Penal Substitution. With over 30,000 different denominations holding drastically different biblical conclusions on basic issues like "salvation." With the simple fact that the Greek words now biblically translated to mean "homosexual" were not translated as such until 1945.[25] With a sure history of countless Christians convinced they held the scriptural truth while committing terrible atrocities in the name of God and biblical faithfulness. How on earth can anyone not be stricken, humbled, and entirely dismantled at the thought that all they hold to be so infallibly true about the Bible could actually be wrong—and not just wrong, but evil?

In fact, the apostle Paul initially concluded that the Gospel excluded the Gentiles—wrong.

John Calvin, the "founder" of Calvinism, believed his theology was so pure and true that it justified the murder of his detractors—wrong.

Early conservative Christian American settlers believed God endorsed the pillaging and murdering of the American Indian—wrong.

Conservative American Christians of the 19th and 20th centuries believed that according to the Bible, blacks were inferior humans who deserved discrimination and a life of brutal slavery, and marriage between a white and black person was an abomination—wrong.[26]

---

[25] The NRSV translation was the first to do this.

[26] "The right of holding slaves is clearly established by the Holy Scriptures, both by precept and example."

Many modern conservative Christians still believe that women are a lesser vessel and should be restricted from certain roles in the church—you guessed it, wrong again.

Come, I beg of you, let us reason together. How many times do we have to be so drastically and demonically wrong until we finally listen to the counsel of the biblical writer who admonished, "...lean not on your own understanding"?

Isn't it, at the very least, pure barbarianism to harbor a default position of condemnation and inferiority when the "clear teachings of the Bible" are clearly not so clear at all? If we can't get something as simple as "salvation" settled and certain, how could one ever become so sure in their "biblical" stances with regard to something so complicated, for example, as human sexuality?

Throughout the New Testament, new experiences were the driving force that led key Christians to ask the question, "Have I read this right?" No, it wasn't some scholarly, exegetical orgy of dissecting a text that inspired the reexamination of a biblical issue, but, rather, new experiences with life, relationships, and flesh and blood that led people like Peter and Paul to deep, theology-altering questions of understanding regarding "what the Bible says."

In fact, it was a sad state of affairs that the Jews, who experienced Pentecost and were the first Christians, did not believe the Gentiles could even receive the Gospel. Talk about inclusion issues, how messed up is that? In fact, the growth of the first church was exclusively of Jewish people. So much so, that Peter had to have an experience with God that led him to reevaluate his reading of a biblical text about clean and

---

-Furman, Richard. "Exposition of the Views of the Baptists, Relative to the Colored Population in the United States: In Communication to the Governor of South Carolina." Second ed. Charleston, 1838. http://eweb. furman.edu/~benson/docs/rcd-fmn1.htm. Page 6.

unclean foods, a metaphoric communication of deeper issues regarding Jews and Gentiles.[27]

Enter Cornelius. Cornelius, a Gentile, was led to Peter because of his rumored spiritual experiences. Peter could not begin to fathom that Cornelius could experience God. But once their bumpers were in the same parking lot, face-to-face, relationship-to-relationship, Peter was blown away by Cornelius' receptiveness and spiritual capacity. After picking his jaw up off the ground, Peter, going against his original reading of the biblical text, shared the Gospel and "Boom! There it is," new life for Cornelius.[28]

Let's just make sure we're all getting the picture here. Until that experience, Peter adamantly believed, along with the Jews, and because of the way they "read" the Scriptures, that the Gentiles had no access to Jesus and the Gospel, and even withheld the waters of Baptism therefore.

Oh, and by the way, the Gentiles comprised 99% of the rest of the world. Yes, that's right, the Gentiles are likely you and me. Thankfully, Peter, Paul, and others had the cojones to ask the question, based on new experiences, "Have we read this right?" and were willing to admit they were wrong.

Truth be told, the more time we spend on our high horses riding people like mules by using the Bible to intimidate them to back our agenda, the more our ears are closed, our hearts are hardened, and life experiences lose their Spirit-led capacity to hold us over the text, demanding we ask one of the most important questions in our spiritual lives, "Have I read this right?"

---

[27] Acts 10:9-16
[28] Acts 10:1-33

So, why are so many conservative Evangelicals insistent on the infallibility of the Bible and their interpretations of it?

Why don't many conservative Evangelical Christians find spiritual strength and integrity in embracing the tensions, ambiguity, limits, subjectiveness, and uncertainties beautifully interwoven into all of the Scriptures?

There's a reason, and it's not pretty.

There's a reason why predominantly conservative, white, male, heterosexual Christians bought into a twisted scriptural understanding of some kind of "manifest destiny" that spiritually justified the conquest, rape, murder, and pillaging of countless Native Americans. There's a reason why a white, heterosexual, male-driven, conservative, Evangelical Christianity led the way in using the Bible in spiritually justifying the slavery, murder, and discrimination against black people, and couldn't bring themselves to acknowledge their highly influential role in these atrocities until 1995. There's a reason why white, male, heterosexual, conservative Evangelicals met in the 1940s and voted to change the words in the New Testament that were long translated as "pedophilia" to now to be translated to mean "homosexual."[29] There's a reason why a white, heterosexual, male-driven, conservative Evangelical Christianity now leads the way in the demonization, marginalization, and discrimination of the LGBTQ community and stands as perhaps the greatest catalyst toward their suicide rates.[30] There's a reason why many conservative Christians claim to be pro-life while, at the same time, they are certainly pro-choice about the Bible—determined to protect their freedom to use every interpretive knife they can contrive to abort countless people into hell, murder their souls with condemnation, and

---

[29] Article: "Evangelicals, Homosexuals, and Child Molesters" -Libby Anne
http://www.patheos.com/blogs/lovejoyfeminism/2013/02/evangelicals-homosexuals-and-child-molesters.html
[30] "LGBT Youth in America's Schools" -Jason Cianciotto and Sean Cahill

yank them out of the womb of God's Grace, slicing and dicing them with sin-labels and discrimination—all while singing songs to Jesus with a self-righteous smirk on their faces. There's a reason why 80% of conservative Evangelicals voted for and elected Donald Trump as President and seemingly will stop at nothing to spiritually justify their ardent support and loyalty towards predatory, sexist, narcissistic, sexually-abusive, bigoted leaders who will promote their Evangelical agendas.[31]

The reason? It's simple—power and privilege—white, male, heterosexual, conservative Evangelical power and privilege. After all, it's really not about the Bible--it's about using a book written by humans about God for playing God in the lives of humanity. It's about power, control, and privilege. Without the infallibility of the Bible and their exclusive interpretive authority, it all blows up in their face and their ability to control and pursue power and privilege is rendered impotent.

See, when people say, "This is what the Bible says," don't let them fool you, what they are really saying is, "This is what I believe the Bible says." One of the hallmarks of religion and large segments of conservative Christianity is to place one's stances on the Bible over their stance with people. Why? For one, self-righteousness finds its wings and people are best controlled with a theology that's black and white and a book that is determined to be unquestionable and inerrant in content and understanding. Yet, ironically, Jesus makes the Bible perfectly errant, highly debatable, and a book that must yield to and be understood in light of the revelation of He who is Grace, the only perfect, inerrant Word—especially when it comes to applying these words on a page into people's lives.

---

[31] Article: "White evangelicals voted overwhelmingly for Donald Trump, exit polls show" -Sarah Pulliam Bailey November 9, 2016
https://www.washingtonpost.com/news/acts-of-faith/wp/2016/11/09/exit-polls-show-white-evangelicals-voted-overwhelmingly-for-donald-trump/?noredirect=on&utm_term=.31143f1331de

The heart of Jesus isn't to control or condemn people with the Bible, but to free people from the misuse of it and the religious who would weaponize it. That's why Jesus never led anyone to a book for anything, but always to Himself. Sit in a room with a Calvinist theologically debating an Arminian, and you'll probably prefer a root canal by the time the whistle is blown. Life, faith, God and people are best understood and related to through the person of Jesus alone. Most anything else is idolatrous religion wrapped in spiritual pride and self-righteousness.

In fact, scan the horizon of Christianity, and you will find that the Bible is largely only "cut and dry" to people seeking the control of another and the spiritual justification of self. For nothing levels people we don't like and creates mountains upon which to judge others like the perfected craft of Christians turning the Bible into a bulldozer. What God meant to be a human springboard to a life-long encounter with Jesus, Christians have turned into a people prod, hoping to corral the world into their religious ideology.

The truth of the matter is the "clear teachings" of the Bible aren't clear to anyone, and everyone knows it, except those who arrogantly claim to know it best. The heights of authority we insist on attributing to the Bible are often sadly equal to the depth of our desires to exert authority over others. "This is what the Bible says" is ultimately our clever way of declaring, "This is what we believe the Bible says, and you need to believe it, too, or else."

Yet, for all our proof-texting and weaponizing of the Bible, the world isn't fooled, and every verse loses its ability to condemn, judge, and breed self-righteousness the moment it is rightly placed under the feet of Jesus who is Grace, the only perfect Word of God.

In fact, when it's all said and done, we don't have to interpret the Scriptures toward inerrancy, racism, sexism, homophobia, transphobia, xenophobia, bigotry, a life of sin-management, God-appeasement, or a tormenting hell for people who miss the mark in loving God in return—we choose to. There are biblically faithful ways of interpreting the Bible that reflect a God of pure Love, Grace, affirmation, and inclusiveness. Yet, sadly, the underlying flames of our prejudice, hate, condemnation, and pride were in our hearts already; we just use the Bible to fuel them and give it all a spiritual glow.

See, people don't dismiss the Bible because of Jesus, they dismiss the Bible because of us. In fact, Jesus came to disarm those who would militarize the Bible and to take back the Biblical narrative about a God who is love and whose message, way, and power is Grace alone.

However, sadly, for many conservative Evangelicals, there are few (if any) verses in Scripture they haven't found a way to weaponize— ultimately seeking to lord, control, and assert themselves over people and society.

Don't believe me? Take a moment to sit at the table of the people that conservative Evangelicals hate, disagree with, condemn, and the issues being harbored that they are so against. Maybe then, you can hear the megaphone of Jesus trying to break through and penetrate the noise blaring in the conservative Evangelical earphones many wear as He whispers, "You have heard it was said, but I say unto you."[32]

During my many years of being a conservative Evangelical pastor, there were numbers of good, honest, Jesus-loving people who questioned my views about the Scriptures, especially when I postured the Bible as being inerrant along with my understanding of it. With clever statements like, "If you don't believe it all, you don't believe it at all," I would seek to intimidate and shame them into compliance. When push came to shove, I would whine about the apostasy happening in the world and how their disagreements with the Bible (and my interpretations) were really a

---

[32] Matthew 5:21, 27, 31, 33, 38, 43

97

reflection of their disagreements with God and their adoption of the carnality of a hell-bound society.

Sadly, I joined significant segments of conservative Evangelical Christianity in worshipping the Bible and my interpretation of it as if Jesus was secondary, or didn't exist at all. Nothing revealed my infantile, pacifier-like dependency on the Scriptures more than when one pulled it from the clenches of my lips, challenging issues of inerrancy, proof-texting, and my weaponizing of its use. Kicking and screaming, I demanded control and would not rest without declaring it infallible along with the exclusive authenticity of my interpretations. For years, my peace and faith were not in Jesus, but, rather, upon the spiritual pacification my worship of the Bible afforded me—forever perpetuating an evil, spiritual adolescence. For no greater evils have come upon the earth than from Bible-sucking Christians like I was, whose faith is solely founded and directed by their scriptural understandings, instead of the person, the only Word of God—Jesus, whose mind we possess and whose Life is ours.

Thankfully, there was perhaps no more important layer of waywardness removed in all my transformation than when I started worshipping Jesus alone, listening to His mind within me, and embracing the Bible as inspired, human words about God in contrast to seeing them as divine, infallible words from God.

One of the most important transitions in one's spiritual life is moving from reading the Scriptures through the mind of the Scriptures written in the pages in front of them, to reading the Scriptures through the mind of Christ, written deep within the pages of themselves. For the mind of the Bible is human-driven, the Mind of Christ is Spirit-driven. One is found in the words written on a page by a writer, the other is found in the words written upon the heart of the reader. One breeds the religious spirit; the other brings Life.

The Bible is beautiful, but not perfect. It leads us into our own encounter with Jesus, but should never become His replacement nor constrict His revelation within in our lives.

The Bible isn't a strict dictation from God of His nature and ways, nor a detailed, infallible diary of His human interactions, but, rather, an organic catalog of important human journeys toward the understanding of life and God's intersection and interactions therein—human understandings that are often imperfect and, at times, even drastically off the mark, painting colors and storylines into a picture of God that are, in reality, far from who or how He truly is. Yet, nonetheless, each giving us a window into the highs and lows, the clarities and the misunderstandings we all experience along the way—each step, right or wrong, filled with the capacity to know Him more fully and live in Him more accurately than at first.

In fact, if the writers of the Bible were infallible in their understanding of God and their interpretation of His actions among them, there would be no need for the Infallible One, Jesus Christ.

If the writers of the Bible perfectly captured the desires of God and His every design for all of life and living, there would be no need for the Perfect One, Jesus Christ.

If the writers of the Bible captured the sum, conclusion, and depth of all that is truth, there would be no need for the One Who Is Truth to reveal it and His Spirit to guide us in it.

In this way, the Bible is intentionally imperfect and incomplete so as to launch us into an ever-flowing river of encounters with the Perfect One— encounters not purposed on gaining complete understanding, but on finding complete rest in the One Who Is Understanding—writing alongside of us our own personal Bible of faith journeys with Him where theology is best learned at the feet of Jesus not in the pages of someone else's experiences and interpretations.

The Bible is intentionally imperfect so it can serve as an antibiotic to the religious spirit that can infect us all, turning us into leatherbound terrorists as we take what God purposed for good and join the Empire in using it for bad.

Read the Scriptures, learn to love them passionately, but only let Jesus (the mind of Christ within you) be the one, true guide of your interpretation, use, and understanding of them. That way, you'll discover over time, all the ways Jesus redefines, reinterprets, and even discards some of what's written—and you should, too.

Perhaps, this is the essence of what is truly authoritative and divinely inspired about the collection of faith experiences we call the Bible—all leading us to encounter for ourselves the Author and Finisher Of Our Faith, Jesus the Christ. In so doing, we embark not upon a slippery slope that steers our theologies into the ditch, but a trail of faith that allows God to reveal Himself more clearly and deeply as we discover there is always more to know and more that He reveals of the expanse of God who is Love.

Maybe, If You'd Just Stop Quoting The Bible At Me…

Yet, still, if you are like me, when I was challenged in my biblical understandings, you aren't convinced. At least, not yet, and perhaps you never will be. You're passionate about your beliefs—that's highly admirable.

When you quote the Scriptures, your desires are most assuredly noble and good-hearted. No one can deny your commitment, resolve, and tenacity towards your faith, the Bible, and a desire to make a difference. To be sure, that was my intention.

Yet, tragically, what I didn't realize was how I was coming across in my use of the Scriptures and some of the messages I was sending in doing so—intended or not. Maybe that's not an important nuance to you, and at times it wasn't important to me, but there are countless people who are desperately trying to call our attention to the repugnant taste our reckless use of the Bible is leaving upon the receptors of their souls--if only we would listen to their plea.

In fact, looking back, I can't believe the terrorism I sowed into people's lives through the use of the Bible: day-after- day, week-after-week, person-after-person. And now that I'm no longer a faithful member of the conservative Evangelical team, I can't tell you how many times people have now knocked on my door with their vicious condemnation, disgust, disappointment, and desire to convert me back—each time quoting the Bible at me to do so.

When this first started happening, I literally wanted to vomit at how terrible it felt to be on the receiving end, knowing I had tormented the lives of countless people in the very same way. I couldn't believe the monster I had become, and what so many had experienced from my weaponizing of the Scriptures. It was then that I truly knew what it felt like to be the victim and, in so doing, came up with the only term that fully described the person I had become and the death I had caused—leatherbound terrorist.

Do you know what it feels like to have the Bible quoted at you? Have you ever experienced the devastation of being condemned, marginalized, used, and hated in such a way that you are led to believe that God is author and communicator of it? Do you have the courage to step outside of the conservative Evangelical Empire and feel the full weight of its evil clamping down upon your soul? Do you have the guts to stomach the bullets and field the shrapnel of what is nothing less than leatherbound terrorism?

This is what it feels like: tenfold—pain, isolation, condemnation, belittling, shame, exploitation, and abuse, to name a few. For nothing mutilates the soul like the highlighted Bible of a conservative Evangelical Christian waiting for someone to devour.

In fact, when you quote the Bible at me, it feels like you care more about winning an argument than winning my heart. Sometimes, it seems like you're inspired most by the prospect of somehow putting me in my place—pacing for the opportunity to engage in debate. With every verse you position to convict, condemn, and admonish, apparently you understand the Bible to be "useful in teaching and correcting" the way a tightly wound parent might deem a paddle to be useful in painfully punishing their child—any love you may intend to communicate is severely lost in translation. In fact, as much as I may desire to conclude otherwise, with every proof text and citing of scriptural support, it feels like the Bible has become, for you, less of a mirror in which to examine yourself, and more of a missile to launch at others.

Maybe, just maybe, if you'd stop quoting the Bible at me, I'd actually start believing you might truly want to know me, understand me, and even love me.

When you quote the Bible at me, it makes me wonder if you really know what you believe. I mean no disrespect, but at times, the way the Scriptures roll off your tongue so automatically and instantly, it feels a bit pre-packaged and cut and pasted—like you haven't taken the journey of authentic believing. The memorization of verses takes only the efforts of our brain and can be a deceptive spiritual veil to an empty life. Meditation requires the soul searching of the heart and personally encountering Jesus. My sense is that people who truly know Him, genuinely wrestle with their faith, and are treading deeply into the Bible, spend far less time in need of quoting it to others and using it to justify their every belief. For the mind of Christ within them has taken the lead, and what they believe is far less a product of simply the Bible saying so, but much more that Jesus has said so in their Spirit.

Maybe, just maybe, if you'd stop quoting the Bible at me, I'd be far more inclined to consider that you're actually speaking from that which Jesus has authentically revealed to you and what He might truly desire to say.

When you quote the Bible at me, I get the sense that you believe you know all the answers. Sometimes, it's even hard to get a word in edgewise. It feels like no matter what I say, somehow, I'm always off the mark or completely wrong all together. For every thought I have, you seem to have a Bible verse cocked, loaded, and ready to counter it. All of which leaves me wondering, if you have all the answers already, why do you position yourself as desiring conversation? Perhaps, you're hoping to change my mind, or simply enjoy hearing the sound of your own. Either way, the more you appear to have all the answers, the more I become convinced you probably don't.

Maybe, just maybe, if you'd stop quoting the Bible at me, I'd hear the sounds of your listening and learning instead of the chalkboard-screeching nails of presumptuousness.

When you quote the Bible at me, it smells of religion, not revelation. No, God never changes, but what He reveals of Himself and how He reveals Himself certainly does. Yet, with nearly every verse you quote, it feels like you are desperately trying to protect and prosper the religious spirit and your long-held beliefs, instead of exuding a humility and openness to encounter fresh revelation. In fact, if I'm honest, It comes across at times as if you're afraid of what God might reveal. It's as if the Bible has become for you, less of a catalyst to encountering Jesus, and more of a replacement for Him. All of which leaves me wondering, if God desired to grow you beyond your current scriptural understandings and interpretations, would He even be able to do so?

Maybe, just maybe, if you'd stop quoting the Bible at me, I'd be far more inclined to believe you possess the capacity for divine discernment and the journey needed for wisdom.

When you quote the Bible at me, I feel like a project. At times, the way you use the Scriptures, it seems like your ultimate goal is my conversion, conformity, and compliance to your beliefs and biblical interpretations. If I have a change of mind or repent of my erring ways in response to your scriptural interventions, a rousing moment of high-fives with your fellow Christians is surely just around the corner. You "caught' me, "won" me, or "discipled" me into your fold, and now I'm yet another "catch" to be mounted on your spiritual mantel. I mean no disrespect in saying so, but it feels like the way you use the Bible is more like a cattle prod than a stable, and I, more of a project than a person.

Maybe, just maybe, if you'd stop quoting the Bible at me, I'd be far more willing to open the gates and consider that you have a genuine care for me and my best interests.

When you quote the Bible at me, I wonder what you're trying to hide. Maybe it's just me, but I have found that those who are constantly quoting the Bible with proof texts, debates, and scriptural arguments are often the ones concealing deep levels of spiritual immaturity, doubts, duplicity, and even carnality. In fact, Satan is described as knowing the Scriptures quite well, all while completely missing the heart of Jesus— obviously. The more you quote the Bible at me, the more I begin to consider, maybe this is all just a big show of biblical smoke and mirrors concealing a cowardly wizard hiding behind a leather-bound, name-engraved curtain.

Maybe, just maybe, if you'd stop quoting the Bible at me, I'd feel a lot more comfortable in extending trust, respect, and credibility.

When you quote the Bible at me, it feels like you're just another one of "them." You know, those Pharisee types that Jesus loved, but aggressively challenged at every turn, were using their understanding of the Scriptures for the condemnation of others and the justifying and puffing up of themselves. In one place, Jesus spoke of spitting repugnant people like this out of His mouth, and, quite honestly, I don't blame Him. Sometimes, the way you quote the Bible at me, it makes me want to vomit, too—if only a simple, right-cheek sneak would do. For it all comes across so pretentiously, my entire being can't help but want to expel it.

See, when Jesus referenced the Bible, He did so, primarily, to reframe it and reinterpret it through the lens of Grace, love, and Himself.

I'm no spiritual giant, but I have a hunch we would do well to follow His example.

Maybe, just maybe, if you'd stop quoting the Bible at me, I would respect you all the more, have a greater desire to give serious consideration to your claims and creeds, and be far more apt to conclude that Jesus is truly working in and through you.

In fact, take notice that the corner of America where there is often the most rampant manifestations of spiritual condemnation, bigotry, and hate, isn't called the Jesus-belt or the Love-belt, but rather—the Bible-belt.

"Pay no attention to the man behind the curtain!"
— L. Frank Baum, The Wonderful Wizard of Oz

CHAPTER EIGHT
Smoke And Mirrors

Sin is a bitch.

We all struggle with it, and fight to untangle from its web, often unaware that the more we twist and punch, the more assuredly it has its grip.

That's why, believe it or not, there is something far more sinister than sin itself that can plague our lives--that is, the religious evil we adopt in hopes of curing it. For the cancer of sin declares its ultimate death sentence over our souls through the self-righteous spirit it can so easily birth within us all. If we just apply ourselves spiritually, have more faith, and summon enough self-control, it feels like freedom is possible. In fact, nothing could be more enticing. To think that victory is just a running start away--it all seems so delightfully doable. This is the seductive allure of Satan's greatest scheme—religion. This is the time-release capsule of perpetual hell that infected my entire being, often finding its way into the areas of our greatest vulnerability for guilt and shame, of which, for me, there were many, but perhaps none more powerful than sexual, given my history of having been abused.

There I was, sitting at that computer in my closet office, face down, in tears. Not only was pornography having its way, but the evil toxins of religion were now beginning to penetrate every gland in my soul. Lifting my head, possessed by the religious spirit fermenting within me, with fists clenched, I bit the lie and determined with all my being that with Jesus at me side, I was going to outrun the demons within me, and become an "overcomer" equipped with a shiny new chapter to bolster my "witness."

What I thought (and had been taught) would bring me the cure to my corruption was the tragic beginning of the systematic murder of all that was true and life-giving within me.

I listened to all the tapes, applied all the prayer formulas, solicited an accountability partner, and even installed protective software. I surrendered my heart and life to Jesus at a level I had never done before. I was pressing in, getting radical, and setting my heart on fire for Jesus. Yet, month-after-month, year-after-year, as much as I wanted to believe otherwise, nothing was getting any better. In fact, it was growing significantly worse (and slowing down my computer). Every time I reached the bottom, I would tap into a rousing message of shame and self-improvement to jumpstart me back upon the religious treadmill of sexual purity. I must have "recommitted" myself a thousand times, never realizing that the more I tried to manage my affliction and perform my way out of it, the tighter the Chinese handcuffs of conservative Evangelicalism became. With no success in the present, no success on the horizon, and wanting with all my heart to please God and master this "stronghold," I quickly learned to deceive myself, fake my recovery, and stow the guilt and shame below as far as I could bury it. All along, giving messages and counseling sessions that passionately spoke of the importance of sexual purity—without even a pause in my step nor a check in my spirit. This was the hollow Christian I was becoming.

Ironically, one of the attributes that initially attracted me to conservative Evangelical Christianity was its perceived determination to take sin super seriously. In my early years, the Lutheranism from which I started my Christian faith and ministry, seemed to gloss over this importance, to the detriment of my life and pastoral ministry, at least, so I was told and believed. At first, it seemed like nothing could be suspicious or wayward about prioritizing sin and becoming skilled at defining it. In fact, haunted by my own daily battles with ungodliness, I surmised this new found focus on sin would enable me to overcome it more successfully in my own walk. Sin is important, and to not take it seriously is a popular contributor to unfavorable outcomes in all of life. Therefore, what could be more essential than to align oneself to a system of faith that has its radar finely tuned to all things sinful?

Sadly, what I was tragically discovering was the dubious smoke and mirrors that conservative Evangelical Christianity hides behind in its relationship with the issue of sin.

For so long, I believed their obsession with it was honorable. I believed their vehement stances against it were necessary. I even convinced myself that their brand of believing held the only true cure for it. Yet when all their religious strategies and formulas for defeating it left me spinning in hopelessness like a breakdancer on crack, I started to have serious questions.

Why on earth do they present a cure for sin that in actuality is the poison that inflames it and gives it life? Why, with such great fanfare and obsession, do they vigorously comb the sands of our culture with their high-powered sin detectors in hand? Why do they seem more than willing to go far beyond a healthy, genuine concern for the ramifications of sin in people's lives to pretentiously reveling in moments where they can point the finger at perceived sin and parade their admonishment of it? Perhaps, most of all, why does it seem that conservative Evangelical Christianity would love nothing more than to have us all convinced that their agenda is altruistically focused on what they perceive to be sin and its negative impact on people and society?

With every question that was pounding down the doors of my religiosity, I was confronted with the reality that there's something much deeper and disturbing under the surface of their sin preoccupation.

Backed into a corner of honesty and firsthand experience, sadly, what I found was this. Conservative Evangelicalism's love affair with the issue of sin isn't about true life change, personal integrity, spiritual growth, or godliness. It's about something altogether evil and diabolical in purpose.

In fact, here's the revelation that saved so much of life. Are you ready for it?

For much of conservative Evangelical Christianity, their obsession with sin isn't about sin at all, and it never has been. Rather, it's about power and privilege—that is, their power and their privilege. Sin has been used, abused, false-flagged, and fabricated into an ultimate distraction away from their primary aspiration and goal—power and privilege.

That's the truth, and until I admitted it, freedom always eluded me.

For if conservative Evangelicalism was truly concerned about sin, several things would be happening that are most certainly not.

First, conservative Evangelical Christianity would be aggressively focused on their own sin, not the perceived sins of others. The teachings of Jesus that call our attention to give personal sin far greater importance than the speck perceived in another, would be given top priority.[33] The primary sounds you would be hearing from conservative Evangelical Christianity would be the continuous cries of their own repenting for the countless atrocities that have been wielded from their system and manner of faith. Statement-after-statement and resolution-after-resolution would declare their continued remorse and commitment to personal change and soul searching. The only thing they could find time and energy to boycott would first be themselves. Thousands would be desperately ridding their lives of gluttony, greed, judgmentalism, racism, sexism, bigotry, legalism, discrimination, imperialism, nationalism, and countless double standards. Churches would be selling their multi-million dollar state-of-the-art facilities and moving to much more cost-effective solutions in order to gain the resources to reach the "least of these" instead of building

---

[33] Matthew 7:3-5

ministry empires and franchising Jesus. Countless churches would be begging for mercy in response to all the ways they have put the color of carpets, the style of music, their personal preferences, the worshiping of the Bible, their spiritual navel-gazing, and the keeping of traditions far ahead of extending the love of Jesus to people. The world would tire of hearing the deafening laments and pleas for forgiveness pouring out endlessly from conservative Evangelical circles—if it was all about sin.

Second, conservative Evangelical Christianity would be communicating far more Grace and kindness. In fact, conservative Evangelical Christians would be ascribed as undeniably being the kindest most gracious people on the planet, trumpeting the message of the pure Gospel of Grace at every opportunity—knowing and teaching that, "It is God's kindness that leads to repentance," and "It's the Grace of God that teaches us to live rightly."[34] Sin would be taken so seriously that pure Grace would be valued as the only solution.[35] Change away from sin would be so important that kindness and Grace would be uplifted and protected as the only catalysts to freedom. All because, nothing else works and we don't have time to waste prescribing the cancer and not the cure—if it was all about sin.

Third, conservative Evangelical Christianity would be truly and completely trusting the Spirit. For the Christian calling isn't to change people, but to love them unconditionally while the Spirit does what only the Spirit can do. In the presence of perceived sin, conservative Evangelical Christians would be doing everything possible to get out of the way of the Spirit and to doubly make sure they didn't serve as a detriment or distraction to the Spirit's work. They would be so sensitive to this movement in people's lives that to potentially error on the side of thwarting God's transformative hand through fostering false guilt, shame, and condemnation, would send shivers down their spine, causing them to value restraint above all else— if it was all about sin.

---

[34] Acts 20:24; Romans 2:4; Titus 2:12
[35] Romans 5:20

And finally, conservative Evangelical Christianity would be unconditionally serving and loving to the extreme. In fact, conservative Evangelical Christianity would be declared the greatest friend a person could have, especially those labeled as "sinners." The way conservative Evangelical Christians generously served, put their needs aside, and extravagantly loved people who have been marginalized, condemned, and demonized would be so world-renowned that people might become attracted to engage in sin or experience religious oppression just for the overwhelming love and selfless serving they would receive in response from conservative Evangelical Christians. In fact, the unconditional love and serving of people deemed to be sinning would become such a priority for conservative Evangelicals, there would be little time for much of anything else to do, dream, or desire—if it was all about sin.

But sadly, it's not, and these actions, values, and attitudes are rarely seen within much of right wing conservative Evangelical Christianity.

Why?

Because, it's not about sin, it's about power and privilege.

For if it were all about sin, there is no clearer example than much of conservative Evangelical Christianity's continued love affair with conservative political leaders and policies that blatantly and sinfully stand against so much of what Jesus lived and died for. From discrimination-to-xenophobia, from greed-to-violence—these hypocritical political and social realities should never happen among people who claim to worship Jesus, but they do. They wouldn't be continually supported no matter their brutality, but they are. Why? Because it's never been about sin, it's always been about power and privilege.

At the end of the day, conservative right wing Evangelical Christianity would love for us all to foolishly believe that their focus and infatuation with sin is bathed in godliness, holiness, and divine intent.

Yet, sadly, what's the bottom-line allure beneath their insistence on biblical inerrancy, especially in the declaration of sin? Power and privilege.

What's behind their aggressive necessity to continuously condemn and demonize the LGBTQIA community as being full of sin? Power and privilege.

What's at the center of their determination to believe in a hell of eternal torture for sinners who believe differently than they? Power and privilege.

What's underneath their mixed-gospel filled with conditions, loopholes, "to do" lists, and spiritual gymnastics in order to overcome sin? Power and privilege.

What's at stake behind their continued manifestation of sexism, nationalism, and elitism? Power and privilege.

Power to condemn, power to control, power to Lord over, power to legitimize their existence, purpose, and actions. Power to spiritually justify hate, and power to manipulate people into their spiritual Borg.

For so much of conservative Evangelical Christianity, it isn't about sin—and it never has been.

It's always been about power and privilege.

The Wizard Behind The Curtain

In fact, the greatest leverage of a drug dealer is in the power of their pills to keep people addicted and coming back for more. In the eyes of much of conservative Evangelical Christianity, sin is big business, and to present the true antidote of Grace instead of the placebo of religious conservatism would be bad for the conservative Evangelical economy.

To my ultimate dismay, as a conservative Evangelical Christian, far beyond my early battles with pornography, I found myself always missing the mark when it came to issues of sin in my life. No matter how much I pressed into Jesus and applied the latest formulas, I could never wrestle down the power of sin, at least not for long. Once I tackled one issue, another one would surface. All of my raising of hands in the air during worship, late-night Bible studies, and accountability partners were proven impotent to rid me of my demons and bad behaviors. In fact, the deeper I committed myself to apply the conservative Evangelical tenets for overcoming sin, the more I had to rationalize my way through it, hoping to put on a good enough face of spiritual growth while inside I was only getting better at duplicity. Nothing was truly improving in my life except my capacity to lie to myself and even others about the true state of my soul and Christian living.

Sadly, what was happening for me, I discovered was happening for countless others, whether they admitted it or not. As I surveyed the landscape, I found that with all of its "to do" lists and prescriptions to grow spiritually through engaging in certain faith behaviors and commitments, conservative Evangelical Christianity was leading the way at imprisoning people to their sin and brokenness, not freeing them.

In fact, do you really want to know the true culprit behind America's moral and spiritual decline? Do you want to pinpoint the true nature and essence of the antichrist in our world today? Look no further than the faith system of conservative Evangelical Christianity, particularly as it relates to sin.

With every inspiring message peppered with new principles for living, lists of behaviors, and passionate admonitions to press in and try harder, we have created strung-out spiritual junkies addicted to the lures of the flesh to perform their way out of the sin and brokenness in their lives through some kind of "partnership" with Jesus. Becoming "successful" for Jesus and overcoming oneself and the trials of life through any kind of personal spiritual performance is the most sinister trap in all the earth—loading people onto the train of sin-management and behavior modification with the promise to bless and emancipate their lives, only to end up in the gas chambers of the ministry of death—the Law.

At the feet of much of conservative Evangelical Christianity, we have nothing less than a spiritual holocaust in our country where the moral decline is ever increasing, all because we have been preaching the cancer, not the cure.

Yet, sadly, this is exactly what conservative Evangelicalism ultimately desires. Why? Because sin and sin-management is big business. It fills churches, manipulates people, sells books, requires revivals, builds altars, and packs conferences. It's the fuel that drives nothing less than the conservative Evangelical Death Star's existence.

That's why the Gospel of pure Grace is quickly dismissed, demonized, and thrown to the curb. With just one drop, Grace dismantles and destroys the Evangelical machine and reveals its nefarious schemes. For pure Grace is the only power of God to handle, manage, and transform brokenness and sin, and the people in which it resides. That's why they despise it. When it's all said and done, it boils down to one thing, and one thing alone—pure Grace is bad for conservative Evangelical business.

So, please, I beg of you, don't waste your life traveling the endless path that once seduced me, push past the tractor beams that hope to keep you imprisoned. Embrace Grace, I'm pleading with you for your freedom. For any other message, prescription, step, action, or invitation is to embrace condemnation, to live in hopelessness, and to deny oneself of the miraculous sin-busting freedom Christ bestows on us through our awakening to Grace.

Thankfully, the true Christian life is not a test, it's a rest. Spiritual growth isn't about becoming someone tomorrow who you aren't today through one's spiritual performance, but rather it's the journey of our actions and attitudes catching up with who we already fully are in Christ—complete, whole, holy, pure, righteous, saved, and lacking no spiritual blessing. This is the foundation of Grace that enables in us and through us all good things, effortlessly—any other foundation is a sinking sand-spiral of death.

In fact, the only issue God has with sin is the negative consequences it can cause in our lives. In that way, it breaks His heart to see us experience pain or extend that pain to others. Sin does not adjust, limit, or change any aspect of God, especially His heart and closeness to us. God knows that the root of all sin is a condemned heart, and Grace, the only cure. His countenance toward sin is one of compassion, sympathy, and a desire to heal the heart through His unlimited kindness and favor. To be cured of sin's grasp is to be overflowing with a consciousness of His goodness and our sure standing with Him as holy, righteous, and unconditionally loved. Sin cannot master a soul that does not first believe it is condemned. Thus, the singular job of the Holy Spirit in our life is to convince us of God's immeasurable goodness and our forever righteousness apart from our performance and secured by His. Anything that persuades you to believe any less of God or any less of yourself is not of Jesus, but rather the religious spirit of darkness commonly being disguised as Light.

Grace has the only disarming power for the compulsion to sin—the removal of all condemnation from the mind and heart. It is the very freedom to sin that Grace affords that ironically renders sin's power impotent to entice. When I truly embrace Grace, no longer can sin serve as a way to punish myself as a form of self-atonement or medicate a condemned heart within me. When condemnation is removed, sin's attractiveness is thwarted and a true self-love emerges that sees sin as contrary to what is good and best for me. Therefore, I turn away from sin, not to appease God or religiously prove myself, but because I have grown to see and love myself as God does—irrevocably and irremovably pure, whole, and without blemish.

This was the revelation that broke the chains of sin in my life and enabled my emancipation. This is the Grace that rendered pornography impotent to rule me. This is the love that would not let me go, especially in my rebellion. Because of Grace, sin can no longer master me with condemnation and the hopeless pursuit of personal holiness and God appeasement. I'm free to live, love, and be loved in return, just as I am.

"Why is it that, as a culture, we are more comfortable seeing two men holding guns than holding hands?" ~Ernest Gaines

CHAPTER NINE

Maybe This Is The Real Reason You Believe Being Gay Is A Sin

He was a talented instrumentalist in our worship team. Though he loved the contemporary style of our music and was open to the freshness of our ministry, he centered his faith on a more conservative Evangelical bent. As an active participant in The Grace Place, a church that I had started a few years after my awakening, he was an integral and valued part of our fellowship.

I had planned a new series of messages in which I would be discussing alternative ways of understanding issues like heaven, hell, the Bible, and homosexuality. As a church, we cast a vision of agreeing to disagree on many matters of the Christian faith with a commitment to love each other in the midst of rich diversity and differing opinions. The week before I was to cover the topic of homosexuality, John cornered me in order to communicate his decision to not attend the service. I asked him why, and hoped to ease any inhibitions he might have. I assured him that he didn't have to agree with me or any of the perspectives shared. It was clear he had a sense that I was going to give a homosexual-affirming perspective on the Bible and was obviously concerned.

At the end of the conversation, I inquired of him once again, "John, you don't have to agree, you can simply listen, you've got nothing to lose, what are you afraid of?"

To that he replied with a saddened look of shame on his face, "I'm afraid you might convince me."

When it comes to the issues of sin, most conservative Evangelicals believe homosexuality is one of them.

As a faithful conservative Evangelical, I used to believe the same, and was certainly not afraid to stand in the pulpit and condemn homosexuals to hell and proudly call any such orientation or behavior a disgusting abomination. Confident in the purity of my doctrine, I had never researched the issue nor built any relationships with people in the LGBTQ community. For all I cared, they were lost, mentally ill people who needed repentance and my anti-gay beliefs regarding the scriptural testimony towards human sexuality were undeniably sound.

That was, until I became close friends with a woman who was lesbian. She did not exude all the stereotypical attributes of what I thought lesbianism would entail. In fact, I was genuinely surprised when she revealed her true sexual orientation to me.

The closer we became, the more I encountered her divine humanity and a spirituality that was nothing less than beautiful and Christ-like. With growing levels of curiosity, surprise, and questioning, I summoned the courage to ask her about her sexuality. Truth be told, it was more like a series of interviews that lasted over the course of several get-togethers. To my surprise, during those intense conversations, I realized that whatever we have in regard to homosexuality in the Scriptures, it wasn't even close to matching the heart, story, and person before me. Despite what you might be thinking, I wasn't trying to have a change of mind or heart, quite the contrary. None of my children or family members are gay, so I had no dog in the hunt. In fact, staying warm and cozy within my conservative Evangelical anti-gay bubble-bath would have been much easier. Yet, I couldn't help but be confronted with the blaring question that forced my face back to the pages of Scripture and the throne of Jesus,

"Have I read this right?" What I discovered over months of copious study and soul searching was that in the end, believing that homosexuality is a sin is not a scriptural requirement nor the only faithful conclusion. In fact, whether I believe that homosexuality is a sin or not, is ultimately a choice.

Maybe for you, you're not exactly sure why you subscribe to the belief that homosexuality is a sin, other than the countless times you have been told, "That's what the Bible says." You want to be loving, accepting, and viewed as a compassionate follower of Jesus, but numerous admonitions from fellow Christians declaring that "loving people doesn't give license to their sin" seem to give you no other alternative posture than one of judgment and distance.

Sure, you're familiar with a few of the verses typically used to condemn homosexuality and those of the LGBTQ community—since childhood, your mind and heart have been seated around the traditional male/female relationships in Scripture as being the only God-approved model for marriage, gender, and sexuality, but that's about as far as your thinking has taken you. Deep down, it's a complicated issue, and quite honestly, you're not always sure what you believe.

Even though you know some LGBTQ people and, perhaps, might even call them friends, moments of belief-questioning or consideration of LGBTQ-affirming views are quickly summoned to a much more comfortable, default position in your faith, "God created Adam and Eve, not Adam and Steve." For you, you're hoping it's as simple and settled as that, and if it's not, it's just going to have to be.

On the other side of the coin, maybe, for you, it's all so perfectly, crystal clear. There's nothing to reconsider, nothing to learn or unlearn. It's a slam dunk, a biblical no-brainer. Not only have you sat under the popular chorus, "This is what the Bible says," you proudly and boldly sing it from the mountain tops. You believe to know every verse relevant to the issues, even citing original Greek and Hebrew words and context. In your mind, heart, and faith, all things LGBTQ are a deplorable, disgusting affront to God and an offensive abomination before the Lord. Maybe you have never held the sign (or maybe you have), but "God hates fags" largely fits hand-in-glove with the bottom line of your faith understanding. Sure, if they repent, change their ways, and adopt your faith views, there's hope. However, until that day comes, "ground and pound" is your perceived divine mandate to wrestle the LGBTQ demons out of our culture and country. No matter the consequences or costs wrought by your anti-LGBTQ angst and rage, you are "right" and everyone else will always be "wrong"—even to the exclusion, excommunication, and potential suicide of your own LGBTQ child, sister, brother, parent, congregant, or friend. In your mind, any other way of seeing things is to author confusion where God created infallible clarity—and you, the God appointed vessel of His authority and truth. If a transgender person were to commit suicide and your secret (or not so secret) conclusions to this tragic event were displayed on your church's worship screen, it might read something like, "They had it coming to them, for the consequences of sin is death."

Well, no matter where you are on the spectrum of believing homosexuality is a sin, I have an honest question from my own transformation regarding this issue.

Are these really the true reasons you believe being gay is a sin? These are the case "evidences" you really want us to attribute to your actions and beliefs? "The Bible says so..." "God hates fags..." "Rethinking my views or considering new information is unnecessary..." and "God made Adam and Eve, not Adam and Steve." Are these the foundational, core-kind of sentiments that make up the sum, depth, and rationale of your thoughts, words, deeds, and creeds regarding one of the most important issues of our time affecting countless God-imaged souls?

With all due love and respect as I truly want to understand and believe the best, if I'm honest, the ruby-slippered Dorothy in me is having a hard time swallowing that pill. In fact, pull back the curtain of your confessions, and I wonder if there's perhaps a deeper Wizard behind the smoke and mirrors of your anti-LGBTQ declarations—and it's not God, the Bible, or spiritual laziness—in fact, I think it just might be… you.

Maybe, just maybe, the real reason you believe being gay is a sin, is because—you want to. When it's all said and done, it's not anybody else's voice or choice—it's yours.

In a Christian church-world where there are over 30,000 different denominations who read the very same Bible you do, and come to thousands of different belief-conclusions on major theological issues; in a Christian church-world where elective misunderstanding and ignorance are seen as legitimate positions instead of serious problems; in a Christian church-world where there are countless, growing numbers of biblical scholars with the same love for Jesus, submissive heart for Scripture, and tenacity for Truth as you, who see the Bible as affirming LGBTQ people, not condemning them; maybe, just maybe, the real reason you believe being gay is a sin is because—you want to. It's not the Bible saying so, it's you saying so.

In fact, if one can be faithful to the sacred Scriptures and yet come to an LGBTQ-affirming view (which you can) instead of condemning, demonizing, and abusing a whole God-adorned population of humans, why wouldn't you? Maybe, just maybe, the real reason is because—you don't want to.

Even when the story of Sodom and Gomorrah is purely about the sins of rape, sexual violence, and inhospitality, in fact, Ezekiel 16:49 declares, "Now this was the sin of your sister Sodom: She and her daughters were arrogant, overfed and unconcerned; they did not help the poor and needy." So, while many want to use this passage to justify holding up a sign that reads, "God hates fags," according to this passage, it might be better stated, "God hates religious fatsos."

Even when Leviticus 18:22 is a clear indictment on acts of humiliation and revenge, as a man goes outside of his natural attraction to women in order to emasculate a man, having nothing to do with homosexual orientation or homosexuality...

Even when in Romans 1, Paul, with no knowledge of homosexual orientation or homosexuality, is clearly condemning those with a heterosexual orientation, which came "naturally" to them, who were acting in homosexual ways out of anger, desire for power, or lust...

Even when the Greek words now translated as "homosexual" were not translated as such until 1945...

Even then, you are determined to quickly conclude that homosexuality is a sin.

Why? Perhaps, because you want to.

In a Christian church-world where many apparently have little-to-no true fear of having a sin lifestyle of blatant, chosen gluttony and greed that potentially even compromises their eternity; in a Christian church-world where virtually none of its participants would ever dare construct nor hold up the sign, "God hates fatsos"; in a Christian church-world that largely has little-to-no restraint in looking the other way regarding its own sins and strongholds; in a Christian church-world where nearly fifty percent of its married adherents end up divorced, and even the "unbiblical" ones are given a free pass;[36] maybe, just maybe, the real reason why you believe being gay is a sin, isn't for fear of condoning it or leading one into hell, but simply because—you want to.

In a Christian church-world that is known for justifying and feeling oh-so-good and righteous about itself through the condemning and demonizing

---

[36] Article: "Baptists Move To Fight Divorce" Rachel Zoll
https://abcnews.go.com/US/story?id=93112&page=1

of people they conveniently deem to be sinning differently than they; in a Christian church-world that largely needs a sin-battle to fight in order to justify its purpose, worth, validity, energy, and existence; maybe, just maybe, the real reason why you believe being gay is a sin is because—you want to. The self-righteous perch from which you're doing so seems to afford you exclusive divine favor, license for anger, and spiritual justification for hate is just too convenient to step down from. Watching porn on Sunday afternoons never seemed so benign as after a rousing, gay-condemning sermon from Romans 1 and 2. It's a drug only Grace can disarm, but you refuse the "reparative" cure. Why? Because—you want to.

In a conservative Christian church-world where community is often centered around the conformity of beliefs and behaviors; in a conservative Christian church-world where in many of its expressions you are either "in" or "out"; in a conservative Christian church-world where to believe differently is often met with a kiss of death—discipline, rejection, marginalization, termination, or just a good-ole'-fashion greeting line of cold shoulders and religious spankings; maybe, just maybe, the real reason why you believe being gay is a sin is because—you want to. The fear of being convinced of LGBTQ-affirming views is just too strong, and the perceived ramifications, just too costly. When the rubber meets the road and you hear the Jesus-call to put the suffering of others above your own—you simply don't want to.

See, at the end of the day, when Toto draws the curtain open, the scheme that was concealed becomes the truth that is revealed—people don't choose to be LGBTQ, but they sure do choose to believe whether it's a sin or not.

In fact, I find it interesting how many Christians proudly proclaim to be pro-life and wear it as a badge of faith-honor, all while, at the same time, they are certainly pro-choice about the Bible—determined to protect their freedom to use every interpretive knife they can contrive to abort countless people into hell, murder their souls with condemnation, and yank them out of the womb of God's Grace and affirmation, slicing and dicing them with sin-labels and discrimination—all while singing songs to Jesus with a self-righteous, anti-gay smirk on their face.

When all the smoke clears, perhaps the real puppeteer behind your anti-gay beliefs finally emerges—it's you. You don't "have" to believe being LGBTQ is a sin—you want to. When all is said and done, the pain of affirmation has been determined to be greater than the pain of discrimination. The call to take up our cross and follow Jesus, perhaps, is a cost you have concluded is too costly to endure. The ego-humbling, faith-reconstructing, soul-examining, human-loving, life-transforming, and courage-requiring invitation of Jesus to put down the nets of religion for the sake of "the least of these" is finally met with what is perhaps the real sum and truth behind your response—"I don't want to."

Maybe, just maybe, this is the real reason why you believe being gay is a sin—it's not God, not the Bible, not spiritual laziness, nor moral purity or responsibility.

But, rather, all because—you want to.

"If you believe that God is good and that He loves you without regard to whom you are or what you do, you will worship Him wholeheartedly. You will praise him with thanksgiving. If you believe He is angry against you, you will come to him with fear and trying to appease his anger. And you don't know when His anger will be over. Such a god keeps you in a perpetual psychological anguish. That is the typical kind of god we usually worship. That is the typical god approved by authority."—Bangambiki Habyarimana, Pearls of Eternity

CHAPTER TEN
To Hell With Your Hell

I'm not going to lie; it scared the crap out of me. I had never been confronted with the creeds of Calvinism, nor had this theology become an issue in any congregation I served. At least not until about 12 years into my ministry. I was scanning the Christian horizon for materials on Evangelism and found my way to the teachings of people like Ray Comfort and Kirk Cameron. At first, their methodologies were attractive as they seemed to bring focus and direct results to engaging the world with Jesus. I purchased the materials, learned their process, and began to implement it in my personal life and throughout our church. As a faithful conservative Evangelical, I had no problem holding people over the fires of hell in hopes of attracting them to salvation, this new-found confrontational approach simply poured gasoline on that strategy.

Yet, the further I traveled down this road, I discovered that the teachings of Calvinism were undeniably behind the scenes. I didn't know much about Calvinism then, but that would soon change.

Calvinism is complicated by design, everybody seems to have their own highly intellectual version and talking points. Yet, one thing is clear, to subscribe to Calvinism is to believe in a god who not only creates a hell of eternal torture, but chooses some (and not others) to go there. In fact, for countless human beings, the very grace that could save them is intentionally withheld by god. Yet, for others, it is given. Whether a person goes to hell or heaven is exclusively by god's eternal decision and not theirs. It has nothing to do with faith, faithfulness, choice, decision, or desiring God. Some are going to hell, and some are going to heaven, and there's nothing you (or they) can do about it. This is the true essence of Calvinism.

Never did I realize the widespread infiltration of this theology into large segments of Christianity. To be sure, it's the family secret behind significant faith movements. Once respected leaders like Francis Chan, John MacArthur, David Platt, John Piper and many others soon were revealed of their loyalties to Calvinism. The more I looked, the more I saw its far reaching tentacles. How could so many people believe in such a dark, evil portrayal of God and eternity?

I studied the subject passionately to the point that it consumed me. Nearly every moment of every day, it won my preoccupation—month-after-month of research. Is my son whom I love so deeply going to hell, and there's nothing that I or he can do about it? Maybe I'm going to hell, too, how can one ever be for sure? I'm supposed to chalk it all up to God's sovereignty, really? This is God's best idea for humanity? I have never come so close to the heart of evil than when I immersed myself into the mind and heart of Calvinism.

Thankfully, after a long and intense wrestling match, Calvinism was revealed of its folly, and I became convinced of its waywardness, but not without setting into motion my profound questioning of the reality and essence of an eternity spent in a lake of fire. Could there be something equally dark and diabolical in regard to my long-held beliefs about hell in general?

For so many years, I never doubted or investigated my conservative Evangelical indoctrination regarding the issue of hell. Neither did I give much emotional discernment to the ramifications of such beliefs, especially as it relates to the entirety of humanity and the required nature of God to create and sustain such a place. It's a convenient privilege to hold fast to the belief in a dubious hell while concluding that only the enemies of your faith and your God will go there.

Yet, chances are, if you're like me, it's a belief you've grown up with all your life—God loves humanity so much that He sent His Son Jesus to die on the cross in order to save us from His eternal punishment of sinners who don't love Him back in return through believing in His Son and repenting of their sins. As the story goes, through His crucifixion, Jesus took upon Himself the punishment from God that we deserve for sin. God required the death of Jesus in order to forgive sin, and personal faith and repentance are how we benefit from that event. Otherwise, the work of Jesus isn't applied to our account, and we are doomed to spend eternity in a place of unimaginable suffering where our greatest wish is to die, but by God's design, we are prevented from doing so—it's hell, and it's forever.

For those who might find this storyline of human redemption difficult to stomach with its dark portrayals of God, the Gospel, and Jesus...for those who wonder how God could claim to be so loving and, yet, act so sinister in not only imagining this kind of hell, but creating it and making the brutal murder of Jesus the only way out of it...for those who dare to look ahead towards the psychotic duplicity of what it might feel like enjoying eternity in the bliss of heaven while your loved ones scorch in unbearable suffering...for those this whole damnation-thing strikes their conscience as being a bit unsettling, unnerving, and confusing—we've been taught a simple fix. Hell is a necessary and natural manifestation of God's divine holiness and justice. In heaven, we will encounter these attributes so completely and fully that any doubts we might have about God or people suffering eternally will somehow no longer haunt us, but, rather, rest peacefully and easily upon our souls. So much so, that in the presence of God who allows for, created, and sustains hell, we will be forever desiring to sing His praises as millions of others suffer unimaginably.

In short, the brutal, violent death of Jesus and a hell of eternal pain and suffering have been handed down to us, unquestionably, as the ultimate reflection of God's character and His best ideas for how to extend and make real His deep abiding love for humanity.

Maybe for you, these popular teachings regarding God's narrative of salvation are a comfortable fit and central to your faith understanding. In your mind, if people go to hell, it's their fault, not God's. God can do whatever He wants, and if Hell is the setup, so be it. Besides, the Scriptures are clear, people have been warned—believe or burn, that's the Gospel. If one rejects Jesus and refuses to heed His commands, they'll get their just reward—an eternity of torture. God is holy, just, and sovereign no matter how vicious and brutal things play out—for His ways are not our ways, who are we to cross-examine the Divine?[37] Therefore, you proudly and boldly declare the reality of a flaming eternity and the glory of God in sending (or allowing) people there who reject Jesus or live disobediently—thanking God it's not you, of course.

Or perhaps for you, as much as you dislike thinking about hell and are even inwardly perplexed by its reality in contrast to a loving God, your understanding of the biblical witness and teachings of Jesus seem to leave you no other choice but to conclude that hell is real, and real people will be spending eternity in some kind of suffering existence that affords no hope and no way out. It's not how you would draw it up, and the whole idea is secretly unsettling to you. When it comes to God's wrath, burning in flames, and the brutal crucifixion of His own Son, you'd just as soon focus on something else and hope it all comes out in the wash. You have your doubts, a lot of questions, and significant uneasiness with it all, but that's about as far as you've taken it.

---

[37] Isaiah 55:8-9

Wherever you are on the spectrum, chances are, without a hell for unbelieving sinners, the foundations of your faith understanding make little sense and largely come crashing to the ground. In your mind, if there's no hell, there's no purpose for Jesus. If there's no hell, there's no purpose for believing. If there's no hell, there's no purpose in being a Christian. If there's no hell, what's the motivation? If there's no hell, what's our message? If there's no hell, what's the Gospel? If there's no hell, what happens to all the effort I've put into my righteousness?

So, as difficult, foundation-shaking, and faith-unraveling as this question could potentially be, I'm still going to ask it—what if hell is nothing like you think?

What if hell (if a place at all) is actually just as Jesus alluded, a literal place (Gehenna) located in Jerusalem, associated with the valley of Hinnom that was used as the city dump where a fire was constantly kept to burn up and consume all of the city's unwanted junk? In fact, the word Gehenna occurs 12 times in the Greek Manuscripts of the New Testament, each time being mistranslated to mean "hell" in several versions of the Bible, even though Jesus used it as a clear reference to a city dump.

What if it's an embarrassingly huge stretch of theological abuse to determine in one moment that the admonition by Jesus to, "pluck your eye out"[38] is certainly not to be taken literally, but, yet, in the next moment, His literal use of "Gehenna" in the same sentence should somehow be unequivocally understood to refer figuratively to a real place in the bottom of the earth where people are tortured by the wrath of God in eternal flames? Really?

What if the other three biblical words traditionally interpreted as referring to a "hell of fire and eternal torment" actually are grossly mistranslated and don't actually mean "hell" at all? In fact, Sheol occurs 65 times in the

---

[38] Matthew 5:29

133

Hebrew Manuscripts of the Old Testament, and it simply means "the grave" (the place of the dead) or "the pit." Hades occurs 11 times in the Greek Manuscripts of the New Testament, and it is the direct equivalent of the Hebrew word Sheol. Thus, it also simply means "the grave "or "the pit." Tartarus occurs only once in the Greek Manuscripts of the New Testament in this verse: "For if God did not spare the angels who sinned, but cast them down to hell (tartarus) and delivered them into chains of darkness, to be reserved for judgment."[39] Notice that God casts the angels (not humanity) who sinned down to tartarus and chained them in darkness, to be reserved for judgment.

What if the single word "hell" we use today and associate as "hell" (a place of fiery, eternal torture) is actually not found in the Bible— anywhere, and in no manuscripts? It's true.

What if, in fact, much of modern Christianity's convenient love affair with a hell of flames, wrath, and demons comes much more from the influence of Dante's "Inferno" than ever could be derived from the true words of Jesus?

What if hell is actually a reality experienced in the presence of God, not apart from Him like commonly taught? In fact, two writers in Scripture describe this very notion: "The same shall drink of the wine of the wrath of God, which is poured out without mixture into the cup of his indignation; and he shall be tormented with fire and brimstone in the presence of the holy angels, and in the presence of the Lamb," and "If I ascend up into heaven, thou art there: if I make my bed in hell, behold, thou art there." [40]

What if hell is not the result of God doing something contrary to His nature (love), but, rather, doing more of it? In fact, the Greek word for "wrath" in the New Testament is the word "orge." Unfortunately, the way this word has been translated has been shaped greatly by our pre-

---

[39] 2 Peter 2:4
[40] Revelation 14:10; Psalm 139:8

existing concepts of God as being angry, temperamental, and hell-bent on punishing. The word "orge" actually means "any intense emotion." It's from where we get words like "orgy" and "orgasm." At its core, "wrath" has to do with a very strong passion—not even associated to anger. In fact, the root of "orge" actually means "to reach out in a straining fashion for something that you long to possess."

What if the wrath of God is not Him pouring out anger, vengeance, or retaliation, but, rather, His furious love—grasping, reaching, shaking to possess every person, that they might experience His Grace?

What if hell is the experience of religious-hearted people who despise the pure Grace of God and His unconditional love and inclusion of all people into Himself and the Kingdom? In the eternal presence of the white-hot love of God forever flowing out as a river from His throne (Daniel 7:10), their souls are scorched with frustration, rage, and torment as their self-righteousness, conditional love, and religious arrogance, bigotry, and intolerance are exposed—stripped, and rendered powerless and evil. For the same Grace and love that will be experienced as heaven by many, will be a sure, torturous hell for some. Jesus forever flips over the tables, yet again, and those whom religion joyously sends to the curb are given a prized seat of bliss, and those whom religion gives elite privilege are found to be pouting and wallowing forever in religious disgust.

What if Jesus didn't die to save us from a white-bearded, angry, and vengeful God, but to save us from a fear-driven, faithless life of believing He is?

What if Jesus didn't die at the hands of a God who required His blood-soaked death in order to forgive, but, rather, at the claws of the religious and their diabolical systems of evil whose chief desire is to murder pure Grace and all its self-righteous destroying, all-including implications?

What if, in the hands of a world dripping with oppression, Jesus, through the cross, chose the way of nonviolence, sacrifice, service, forgiveness, inclusion, and unconditional love to model and manifest the Kingdom that was already eternally established by His Grace?

What if Jesus didn't die to forgive us, but to manifest to the world that God already had, long ago in the realm of eternity?

What if God isn't schizophrenic after all—harboring unconditional love for humanity one moment and eternal hate the next?

What if the truth is, you can't reject Grace—you can't stop its presence, pursuit, favor, or blessings over your life or that of any other, you can only love it or resist it? Loving, believing, trusting Grace fills your life with heavenly rest. Not loving, believing, and trusting Grace fills your life with a hell of frustration, self-righteousness, bitterness, religiosity, judgmentalism and angst—as long as you desire, even for an eternity.

What if God isn't an insecure, limited, and codependent parent, whose capacity to save, love, and forgive are restricted to and governed by the obedience (or disobedience) of His children—thus, making them the Lords of the future, not Him?

What if God never changes—He is love through and through, forever and always, no matter what or who?

What if the presence of alternative, biblically-faithful interpretations regarding one's understanding of hell and God's connection to it, back you into an interpretive corner, so much so, that if you believe in an eternal hell of torment and torture for the unbelieving and a God who would author it, you are doing so solely by your own choice?

For the results are in—history paints the picture. We Christians have been drastically wrong before—wrong about racism, wrong about equality, wrong about violence and war, the list keeps on growing.

What if we're wrong, yet again?

If I'm wrong, then God will most certainly go ahead, around, and over me in a divine, full-court-press to scare the hell out of the people I'm misleading—literally. For there's nothing about me or my message that the Holy Spirit is powerless or unwilling to usurp. Any wayward guidance on my part can easily be reversed by the omnipotent leading of the Father. I would boldly stand before the Throne having exaggerated the goodness, love, and Grace of God—if ever that could be a thing.

But, if *you're* wrong, you have participated in nothing less than the evil demonization of God and the sheer blaspheming of His Spirit. You've allowed a spiritual laziness, vulnerability to religious brainwashing, and twisted comfort with the notion of people going to a torturous hell and a God who would create it, to win over your heart, mind, thinking, attitudes and actions. You have leaned on your own understanding of the Scriptures to the spiritual abuse of others—imprisoning them into a life of fear as they are raped of their capacity to know the joy, freedom, and peace that comes from awakening to God who is love, Jesus who is Grace, and the Gospel that is truly good news for all.

"Paradise is the love of God, wherein is the enjoyment of all blessedness... I also maintain that those who are punished in Gehenna are scourged by the scourge of love. For what is so bitter and vehement as the punishment of love?"—St. Isaac the Syrian [41]

"The flames of heaven will be hotter for some than the flames of hell could ever be"—Dallas Willard "The Divine Conspiracy"

---

[41] Ascetical Homilies I.46, pp. 357-358

"Grace is the celebration of life, relentlessly pounding all the non-celebrants in the world."—Robert Capon, *Between Noon & Three: Romance, Law & the Outrage of Grace*

"Intense love does not measure, it just gives."—Mother Teresa

CHAPTER ELEVEN
The Real Reason I Don't Go To Your Church

I have to admit, I've been that pastor. The one who loves the idea of church more than the reality of it. I've been the pastor whose tubes of self-worth and significance were desperately connected to church growth and ministry fame. I've been the pastor who saw people as a means to an end—the expansion of my own conservative Evangelical personal ministry empire. I've been the pastor who viewed church as a superior gathering of primarily white, male, heterosexual people whose job it was to indoctrinate an inferior world. I've been the pastor who, while secretly harboring my own litany of sins, took great pride and solace in pointing out and confronting the sins of others. I've been the pastor who became skilled at spiritually rationalizing the use of people for my own selfish agendas. I've been the pastor who had no restraint nor pause in condemning people to hell, threatening the uncooperative with church discipline, and requiring the disobedient to leave. I've been the pastor whose ultimate concern for people only truly went as far as it furthered the preservation and fruition of my conservative Evangelical, imperialistic ministry ego. To my shame and deep regret, I've been the pastor whose every step left a footprint of white, male, heterosexual privilege, pretentiousness, arrogance, elitism, bigotry, and intolerance--if only I had seen it sooner.

In fact, there's a long list of people who line the halls of my memory that have been unjustly condemned, hurt, discarded, and abandoned in the wake of my conservative Evangelical ministry. Countless have come to the footsteps of the churches I have served longing for the healing that comes through Grace alone, only to be shackled with guilt, shame, and the hopeless pursuit of religious rule-keeping.

Leatherbound **Terrorism**

Her name was Tammy, a caring mother whose teenage child was filled with rebellion. She was at a complete loss for what to do next. It seemed like every parenting strategy was falling short. My conservative Evangelical counsel to her was to send her son to the curb so as to feel the full weight of God's displeasure for his actions. I cleverly wrapped my advice in the package of a tough "biblical" love that required her to change the door locks and cut off all communication with her only son until he cleaned up his act. In the end, that only made matters worse, and she soon left the church with an increased hopelessness.

His name was Bruce, he told me he was inviting a Muslim woman and her gay son to church. He pulled me aside and politely asked about the message that I would be giving on the day they would be in attendance. I suspected he wanted to make sure they would feel welcomed and safe. Yet, the week prior, during my message preparation, my conservative Evangelical talking points couldn't be subdued nor contained from licking their chops. That Sunday, in the midst of my message, I made sure to sprinkle in several lines that communicated the reality of hell for non-Christians and the abominations of homosexuality. While the high-fives were in plenty from the choir, they could not overshadow the broken hearts and souls of Bruce and his guests as they left the church that morning, never to be seen again.

His name was Barry, he was on staff at my church. It was discovered that he had been unfaithful to his wife. With little patience to listen to his story or untangle the issues, my conservative Evangelical reflexes quickly kicked in to assertively handle the scene. I sat him down, swiftly asked for his resignation, and admonished him that until his repentance was louder than his sin, he had no future within the church. In the end, he left (which was my ultimate hope) and so did his wife, never to be heard from again.

See, one of the greatest awakenings one can have in regard to conservative Evangelicalism is its capacity to deafen our ears to the cries of good people and to grant us a nose-blindness to the smells of our own religious stench. If we'd only learn to listen, there is so much to learn. Yet, it's that learning of which we are afraid because of its call and capacity to require change. Sadly, "Church" has long been resistant to listening, and, therefore, to learning what truly needs the renewing and healing power of transformation within.

Like a drunk who would rather die than to embrace the sobering cure, modern American Christianity is willing to risk her future in turning a deaf ear. For we have fallen so far from Grace that people have to shout to be heard, and, even then, they do so only to be shamed.

So many, like Bruce, Tammy, and Barry have countless stories of their encounters with the darkness of conservative Evangelical Christianity. In desperation and disillusionment, they are crying out to be heard.

Yet, theirs are the very voices we so vehemently refuse to hear.

Until now, if you are willing.

For in the sentences and paragraphs ahead, they will speak. In fact, what you will read are the truths we so often refuse to admit and the poignant wisdom we so often refuse to allow influence.

I challenge you, bend your ears to the real reason why countless growing numbers of people are leaving "church" or never coming in the first place. What you will hear could change your life.

If only I could have heard it sooner, it would have spared so many within mine.

To those who have ears, let them hear the voice of good people for whom "church" has not only become irrelevant, but devoid of goodness and the heart of Jesus…

The Real Reason I Don't Go To Your Church

No, it's not the music style, the lighting, or the programs.

No, it's not that I'm lazy, disinterested, or bent towards worldliness.

In fact, I care deeply about spiritual things, long for community, and have a generous heart for serving people.

With your professional branding, elaborate worship staging, cultural savviness, and groups for nearly every interest known to humanity, I can tell that you are feverishly trying to crack the code and leverage me into your church gatherings. Even your ministry conferences, flowcharts, and mission statements are centered around somehow influencing me into your kingdom. Like Captain Ahab tempestuously traversing the oceans for the prized moment his harpoon punctures the elusive whale, it's obvious you long for your efforts to be those that heroically pierce my heart with salvation, lure me into your faith community, and set me on a course to believe and act as you do, all to the praise and admiration of those that align with you spiritually. I see your noble intentions, I really do—all are efforts I truly appreciate.

Yet sadly, the real reason I don't go to your church still eludes you— perhaps because the answer can't be bought, programmed, built, diagramed, staged, earned, envisioned, emotionalized, focus-grouped, or even prayed into existence. For all the chumming of my life with every strategy, program, and event that could possibly ever be imagined, you're still yet drastically missing the one ingredient for which my heart and soul hunger the deepest, and could even render them captured. In fact, the one and only thing that truly matters is the very thing rarely ever heard amidst all your ministry chatter—love.

See, the real reason I don't go to your church, subscribe to your faith understanding, or connect with your spiritual community is actually because of you—you don't truly love me. I'm sorry if that hurts, but I can't deny my experiences and the feeling within me.

If I'm honest, which I hope you want me to be, the one thing you so desperately want me to see and believe about your god and your faith establishment is the very thing I don't see established in you—it's love—and it's oh so very clear, you don't truly love me. With all that your faith, church, and Christian life has become to you, the one thing that hasn't become of you is the one thing that is so glaringly missing—a simple, true, genuine, unconditional love for me.

The real reason—no matter what you might be tempted to conclude. It's not about your god, your buildings, your beliefs, or your community. It's actually all about you— that you don't truly love me. I mean no disrespect, and I'm sure these words aren't easy to hear, but they are the truth of how I see it, as do so many others.

For if you did...

You wouldn't even think of putting your rights, comforts, and privileges above mine. Rather, you'd be laying them down for me.

You wouldn't care so much about bathrooms, wedding cakes, and movie scenes. Rather, you'd be pushing aside every obstacle and looking for every opportunity to simply serve me.

You wouldn't shame, discard, and condemn the people I love, no matter who they be. Rather, you'd love them thoroughly and completely, no less, simply because you love me—you know, like Jesus.
You wouldn't see me as a spiritual project to stuff upon your mantel for all your friends to see, but, rather, as a wholly divine person already redeemed, simply longing for an awakening—you know, like to the Jesus already in me.

You wouldn't say selfish things like, "I'm praying for you" as you pretentiously look down your pointed nose and flaring nostrils and determine that I'm not all that I should be. Rather, you'd vehemently commit your heart to truly understanding, knowing, and loving me—and that, unconditionally.

You wouldn't want to "reach" me, "win" me, or "grow" me into becoming some robotic, spiritual zombie who believes, looks, and acts mostly like you. Rather, you'd want to love me into the God-adorned person who believes, looks, and acts exactly like the true me, living life as "I" should—in freedom, with only the Spirit guiding me, not you. For don't you have enough navigating to do in your own life to necessitate in you the trusting of God with mine?

Your theology and Bible understanding wouldn't be the idolatrous, unmovable, and inerrant foundation upon which you lean, pompously standing as one who holds all the "clear teachings."

Rather, your humility would give way to a love of me that would prevail above all things and become the one and only thing. It would be your vision, denominational mantra, and your ultimate dream—convinced that in all you do for me, you are in fact doing so as your highest and most important way of loving and honoring Thee—you know, Jesus.

You'd be listening, learning, and looking for any reason, excuse, or loophole to affirm me—no, not that there needs to be. That God loves, accepts, and delights in me simply because I breathe, would be more than enough—because that's the heart of Jesus.

Your default bent, beliefs, and creed would all center on Grace, love, and human equality, not jamming down my throat something you have in your privilege that you believe I need as a remedy to what you see as my depravity. For who do you think you are, anyway? You don't even know me.

You'd trust the goodness of God so much that potentially erring on the side of unconditionally loving me would not only be deemed as non-threatening in your heart and mind, it would be concluded to be an impossibility. For with a God of more than enough, who could ever love too much?

Perhaps, most of all, you wouldn't say ridiculous, careless things like, "The reason I point out your sin is because I love you," and then expect me to actually believe it—if only I could keep the vomit from dripping out of my mouth. Rather, you'd be begging me to hear one thing, and one thing above all things, "I love you is the reason I love you." "Pointing out sin is the job of the Spirit, it's not for me." "For who am I, but one who is just like you—not better, only different."

Yet, sadly, you apparently don't trust Grace to guide, teach, correct, empower, and be all-sufficient, which is perhaps the sole reason why yours is a love that is so alarmingly love-deficient.

Please understand, I'm not trying to be disrespectful, hurtful, or flippant with my words. But this is the kind of truth that so desperately needs to be heard and seen.

You want to change me; I just need you to love me. You want to convert me; I just need you to love me. You want to confront, castigate, correct and conform me; I just need you to love me.

There is nothing in all my heart and soul that couldn't be overcome, if you'd just truly and simply love me—unconditionally. But sadly, you don't—and even more tragically, because of your faith understanding—it seems you won't.

Truth is, I don't need to know anything more about your god or your faith community, because I see everything I need to see—in you, already.

With all due respect and appreciation, you can have all your services, traditions, events, conferences, retreats, revivals, groups, clubs, books, movies, schools, buildings, programs, prayers, and music, because I know true love when I see it—and tragically, I just don't see it—in you. It's going to be very hard to convince me that the god atop your steeple truly and deeply loves me, when it's all so crystal clear, from the tippy top to the depths of your own being, a love cannot be found that truly loves me—unconditionally.

This is all the reason I need to know or ever show as to why I'll never want to be a part of your church, your faith understanding, or your community.

The real reason?

You.

You don't truly love me.

This Is What It Feels Like To Be "Loved" By You

For, in the end, any love that you have for me doesn't feel like love at all, sadly.

In fact, I wonder if you know what it truly feels like to be "loved" by you, and to interact with your faith understandings and pursuits.

To be sure, there are many in your faith tradition who are pursuing love with great ambition, but it feels like any love that's given is mainly because, at some level, you kind of have to—all seemingly a part of your faith obligations and spiritual mission. I am sure your heart is real, but it feels like you love me more as a project than a person, with an overall goal to "disciple" me into thinking, believing, and behaving just like you. You call it transformation, the manifestation of a God who loves me

148

enough to "meet me where I am, but not leave me there"—but I am not even sure what that really means, or if it's really true. I'm thinking it might be as simple as God just loves me, period—which leaves me wondering, why doesn't it feel like you do, too?

To be sure, conservative Evangelical Christianity can taste so wonderful when you fit snug into the mold, but it can also feel like a sure kind of hell when you don't—smiles to greet you at your face, surface pleasantries all around, but twitch with a wrong move—knives ready to stab you in your back, pushed to the outside, and even left to drown. The requirements to keeping good going in a relationship with you feels like a tireless game of making sure one plays by all the rules, completes all the steps, and meets your every expectation—otherwise, a clear message is surely in the mail, "We love you, but you're falling short, repent or be removed."

Oh, yes, I understand the idea of divine-authored, corrective conviction and the displeasure that can entail. It's an integral part of your faith system and how the Jesus of your understanding impacts and transforms the world. But this is not about objecting to an appropriate dose of divine discipline, but, rather, the hurt, shame, and harm that's caused by your faith prescriptions and interventions. For divine correction carries with it a kind of pleasurable discomfort as It begins and ends with Grace, kindness, humility, and unconditional acceptance—and thus, what hurts in the process is not the correction, but the regret of not seeing and embracing all the love, forgiveness, acceptance, kindness, and Grace that is already ours in Christ, so much sooner. That's why so much of your discipling and speaking your "truth in love" only feels like pain and punishment as it's completely devoid of the very Grace and truth that saves and makes the broken whole—for punishment never made anyone holy.

I wonder, do you know what it feels like to be shunned—the facial displeasures, the flippant remarks, the disapproving stares, the dissociations, and marginalizations? Do you know what it feels like to be labeled as lesser, inferior, and even evil, particularly by those who declare themselves to be so spiritual and echo the voice of the Creator? Do you understand how your "hating my sin," but loving me as a "sinner" sucks the life out of my soul, condemned by your words as a second-class citizen?

Rejection, shame, disgust—do you know what they feel like when wielded from the visceral of another human?

Where is the discrimination in your life? Where are the toilets you have been banned from using? Where are the cakes that you have been refused? Where are the church fellowships and leadership positions from which you have been deemed disqualified? Where are the parents that sent you to the curb as illegitimate and no longer their true child? Where have we seen you dehumanized to the point of suicide, all in the name of Jesus and biblical faithfulness? Where are the gallows from which you have been hung for simply having a different color of skin? Where do we see you doing more listening than lecturing—more serving than judging?

To be loved by you feels like living in a circus of constantly created wars against enemies you desperately need to exist with for the formation of dire solutions for problems that aren't even real. It feels like you believe yours is a privileged faith that entitles you to special treatment—that you have deemed yourself as being better than the rest and possessors of the inside scoop to all that is Jesus, God, the Bible, and truth.

It feels like you have little to no sense of how much your words impale and your displeasure tortures and kills. Your faith brand imprisons so many in a spiritual maze from which they can never find a way out, upon a scale on which they will never measure up, and within a race in which they can never cross the finish line. In fact, if there was ever a move by the Spirit to improve me, all your conditions, religious prescriptions, and condemnations would surely eclipse it.

I can't help but feel like you are intentionally spinning the Bible towards restricting, restraining, and putting conditions on God, love, and the true freedom and life Jesus brings. It feels like any blanks left in Scripture are always filled in with the most negative, condemning, legalistic, and conditional conclusions possible—not to mention all the ways you allow a pass on your own biblical sins while judging harshly those who sin differently than you.

It feels like you want to hate so much more than Jesus and the Bible are telling you to do so.

It feels like you are much more in love with your stances on the Bible, than in love with standing with people.

It feels like your love of justice is much more like a love of "just us."

I long, so desperately, for the day when you will love me "as is" and all the same if I never change to your liking, but I am grieving the loss that sadly this day will likely never come.

For this I surely know, until our theology is Love, we will always be leaning on our own understanding to the detriment, and even destruction, of other people.

My friend, may I suggest, a new absolute is coming and has already long been here—Grace.

For the non-judgment day is upon us, because all is finished, forgiven, and made whole by the Father through the Son.

And, yet, it feels like, to you, this is bad news, as much as Jesus died to make it good.

Leatherbound **Terrorism**

It feels like you want hell, judgment, condemnation, discrimination, lines, labels, battles, distance, and differences more than Jesus or the Bible could ever desire or deem so.

I mean no disrespect, nor look away from my own imperfections and failures; I just thought there could be a chance you might want to know...

This is what it truly feels like to be loved by you—which, for so many, has us truly questioning if it's really love at all.

"Anyone who does not love does not know God, because God is love." -1 John 4:8

"If I speak with human eloquence and angelic ecstasy but don't love, I'm nothing but the creaking of a rusty gate. If I speak God's Word with power, revealing all his mysteries and making everything plain as day, and if I have faith that says to a mountain, "Jump," and it jumps, but I don't love, I'm nothing. If I give everything I own to the poor and even go to the stake to be burned as a martyr, but I don't love, I've gotten nowhere. So, no matter what I say, what I believe, and what I do, I'm bankrupt without love."—1 Corinthians 13

"Something amazing happens when we surrender and just love. We melt into another world, a realm of power already within us. The world changes when we change. The world softens when we soften. The world loves us when we choose to love the world."—Marianne Williamson

CHAPTER TWELVE
Dear Conservative Evangelical Christianity I'm Sorry, I Just Can't Do It Anymore

The many layers of conservative Evangelical Christianity that had long been suffocating my heart and soul took years to be removed. With each step, new levels of deception were revealed and exposed to the power of Grace. Though there are still moments where certain things can have a triggering effect on my emotions and memory, there was a point where I could finally close the entire book and walk away.

Perhaps it was during our trips to China to adopt two of our daughters when we discovered the incredible risks and sacrifices Christian Chinese people made daily for their faith in Christ in comparison to a consumer-driven American Christianity that prioritizes the color of carpets, stage-lighting, worship fashion, and having a golf-cart to drive one's lazy, spiritual, fat rear-end from their car to the steps of the church.

Perhaps it was the intoxication of Grace that unleashed my soul, freed me to love fully, and opened my eyes to the God of pure affirmation. Oh, how I tried to resist its unstoppable capacity to rest my doubts, disarm my insecurities, and empower my sense of self. In the end, the freedom to be fully me, fully believe in a God who is Love, and celebrate humanity without restraint proved to be far beyond my strength to deny.

Perhaps it was the blood and tears of countless people that my heart finally tasted after years of ignorance and callousness, whose lives had been devastated and discarded exclusively at the hands of conservative Evangelical Christianity.

The list goes on for miles of all the emotional, spiritual, and theological bricks laid before me that paved the path to the ultimate crossroads in my life. It was there that my honesty won over and my heart could do nothing but conclude, "I just can't do it anymore."

I'm sorry conservative Christianity, I can't--I'm finished, I'm done.

They say you have to earn your way out of a marriage by doing everything possible to save it; otherwise, you're abandoning the relationship prematurely and without integrity. Well, in regard to my twenty-year marriage to conservative Evangelical Christianity, I tried. I really did.

.

As you know all too well by now, having read this far, I wanted to fit in, to be a shining star of conservative faithfulness lighting up dark skies. The dream of being successful for Jesus and gaining the gleam of His eye seemed like the apex of all pursuits. I could feel good about myself as I strapped in and revved the engines of the Monster Truck named "Conservatism," enjoying a kind of favor that positioned me above a world of sin-obstacles and rebellious human traffic—it was perfect. With conservative Christianity, there was a stage upon which to spiritually perform, a predefined system of belief to simply absorb and plug in, and a self-validating mission to assimilate everyone and anyone who would listen and buy in. It was all so cut and dry—a faith that was calculable, concrete, and clear in defining who was in and who was out, who was faithful and who was not, and who was right and who was wrong.

Yet, things were changing, finally and completely. A revelation welling up from my soul of a different way of believing and living had shown itself to be an unstoppable force. I couldn't deny the air that I was breathing for the first time and the life it was giving—Grace had awakened me.

No, it still doesn't all add up in my mind like ducks marching in a row, but it doesn't have to when it's all adding up in my heart and soul.

It's not that I don't love you anymore—I do. It's not that I don't accept you without conditions—I do. It's not that I don't believe you are filled with good intention and tremendous, God-adorned worth and value—I do.

I'm sorry conservative Evangelical Christianity, the bottom line is this—I just can't do it anymore.

I Can't See People As Being Inherently Evil And Lost

Something inside me has drastically changed, and I can no longer see people in the flesh, but only as thoroughly in Christ.

It takes so much work and negativity to constantly be viewing the world as intrinsically depraved and evil, as if humanity has the power to make bad all that God has fundamentally created good. Is God's craftsmanship so poor that He could do no better? My heart and soul tire of fighting the hands of the Creator, trying to drag the core nature of humanity down to the depths of my religious insecurities and self-righteousness.

In fact, I've come to learn that Grace is the great equalizer—none of us are better, only different. That's why the religious conservatives sought to kill Jesus and this, His message. When we are all equal before heaven, there can be no controlling, condemning, and fear-driven coercing. We are all loved and accepted equally by the Father—all of us in Christ from the very beginning. Faith is merely awakening to all that has already been given—Grace. People are good, whether they believe incorrectly or behave differently. This is the way Jesus sees all creation, the entire expanse of humanity—I just want to live my life seeing people the way He does.

How beautiful the world is through the eyes of Jesus. People watching takes on a whole new dimension of divine recognition. If only I would have discovered this so much sooner.

The very same people to whom I would once turn down my nose have now become the very people whose feet my heart longs to washt, not because I see them as dirty, but because in the washing of their feet, my soul is cleansed as we celebrate our mutual humanity. In fact, in the presence of those I would have deemed to be lesser, I now find myself having deep respect and seeing far more Jesus in them than in myself.

Isn't that a beautiful desire straight from the throne of heaven, to be free to see beauty everywhere and in everything? What could possibly go wrong with having the highest view of all of God's creation and the quality of His artistry?

It's an amazing thing how Grace can shift and completely turn over the tables concerning whom we deem to be the enemy. People who I once stood against are now the subject of my solidarity. People who once enjoyed the favor of my religious conformity, now feel the sure resistance of my loyalty to Grace.

I mean no disrespect in saying so, but my soul has awakened to the sure reality that to be "of the world" [42] is to now be far more connected to the holy than to be "of conservative Evangelical Christianity." There is no place that I would rather be than joining with the eyes and heart of Jesus to see His presence in, with, and under all things. For all is sacred and all are sacred—Jesus defines everything.

My friend, this is the revelation that intoxicates my entire being with Grace to the point of no return. I've tasted and seen that people are good,

---

[42] John 15:19; 1 John 2:15

because God is good and He's a damn good Creator. I don't have to spend my life sitting in the judgment seat with a disposition to be against the world. I now sit in the couch of Grace with a new heart bent on embracing the very people I once so vehemently condemned. For in doing so, I find the Jesus in me, the Jesus in them, and the freedom to finally be alive in Christ.

What about conservative Evangelicals? Aren't they beautiful, too?

Yes, indeed, they most certainly are which is why (believe it or not) you'll find me at times on Sunday mornings playing piano for a local, independent, conservative Evangelical church. Not because I agree with nor support their pursuits, but because I am called to serve and see God's redemptive watermark upon all things, even those I might discern to be the enemy of much that I hold to be true.

I'm sorry conservative Christianity; I just can't do it anymore.

I Can't Support A Consumer Driven Christianity

To think that I was the pastor who put style over substance, church growth over people, and my ego over the best interests of others is a sobering revelation. I can remember some of my first megachurch experiences and how intoxicating the proposition of ministry fame felt as the needle of seeker-sensitive visioneering entered the veins of my narcissism. Every conference and gathering of pastors was, at best, a corporate-styled symposium on how to make sure your church and your leadership not suck like all those little churches and behind-the-times pastors and, ultimately, a pissing contest to showboat whose ministry was bigger.

During one such meeting of local conservative pastors, as we all sat in a cute little circle, I was the last to be questioned about the status of my church. I had just started a very modern ministry named *Quest 419*. We were growing, but not at the rate of others. I felt ashamed when I couldn't report the kind of church growth statistics that would validate my skills and gain the respect of my peers. In fact, when I was asked to describe our Sunday morning service, I had to announce that we didn't even meet on Sundays, but only on Friday nights. You could feel that air being sucked out of the room. The leader of the meeting, in his well-pressed suit and tie, quickly questioned me further, "Well pastor, what in the world do you do on Sunday mornings?" To that I replied, "Make love to my wife."

Sadly, as I left that meeting, as wicked-awesome as that moment of rebellion was, my selfish determination to become the next pastor to gain the adoration of unprecedented ministry success only grew. My mind was made up, God gave me a "big" vision for a "big" church purposed on "big" things for the Kingdom, and if in the end you couldn't get on board, you were eventually cast aside. I can't tell you how many good people I politely (and not so politely) discarded because they weren't falling in line. All, of course, in the name of Jesus and trailblazing for the Kingdom, with plenty of spiritual rationalizations to pave the way.

To be sure, my heart is filled with repentance and regret for all the ways I contributed to the consumer-driven mindset that plagues much of Christianity and the relationships that were lost in the balance. I was a large part of the problem and a sure enemy of the solution.

For all the books, buildings, blogs, branding, conferences, concerts, movies, ministries, jewelry, t-shirts, stage-lighting, bumper-stickers, worship bands, cheesy, comic, sans-font-ladened Facebook memes, and church groups and activities, who have we become? I dare say, not nearly as sacrificial, serving, and loving as we are consumer-driven in our faith. In fact, the greatest passion inducer in many churches is, sadly, the conflicts that center around the style of worship. Nobody prays harder, studies the Bible more, and gets more involved than a Christian who is trying to assert and defend their personal preferences in church. From what I'm learning, the way of Jesus was sacrifice, not spiritual self-absorption—I just want to live my faith in a way that gives and contributes, not consumes with a rampant kind of spiritual appetite bordering on addiction.

Trust me, it was a hard habit to break with all the allures of Christian commercialism, but Grace has won me over and freed me from the franchising of Jesus and an addiction to personal ministry empire building that's rampant in every segment of American Christianity. I can't believe how much time I spent sucking on the cold, bitter nipples of conservative Evangelical ministry "success." What a true waste of time, spirit, and energy, leaving a taste in my soul I can't believe was ever appealing.

For there is no greater centering for ones ministry and life than to firmly conclude that Jesus is enough—period, full stop. I wish I could give it to you, because there's an unmatched freedom that comes from completely disconnecting one's value, worth, success, and spirituality from the treadmill of American Christianity and its corporate church culture of ministry fame, greed, elitism, and empire building.

I know these words will be hard for some to hear, but so many of the things that were once appealing about church in America now thoroughly disgust me. The dead branches have been cut and the stump has been laid bare. My heart is saddened and filled with deep compassion for those Christians and pastors who have been sucked into the black hole of a success-driven, corporate, narcissistic, elitist church culture overflowing within much of American Christianity. To see their spouses, children, health, relationships, and integrity being swallowed whole by the jaws of church and ministry is a nightmare that I sadly experienced for myself that now brings tears to my eyes to see happening in the lives of countless others.

Thankfully, Grace has carved a path towards freedom where, for me, Jesus is finally enough. In all the unhealthy ways that conservative Evangelical Christianity once seduced me, I don't need church, fame, success, buildings, book deals, ministry, or applause to fuel my identity and establish my worth. In fact, in all the ways one has to sell their soul, I don't want any of it, none of it at all.

I mean no disrespect, but I now find more community, the presence of Jesus, personal significance, and an experience of authentic worship outside of church than I ever did within. And, quite frankly, I am perfectly at peace with that, and I have this sense that Jesus is, too.

I'm sorry conservative Christianity, I just can't do it anymore

I Can't Live With One Eye Open In Fear Of A Psychotic Deity

There is perhaps no greater hell than living your life in fear of a god who is believed to use punishment to bring about holiness. To conclude that the use of divine condemnation, shame, and retribution are God's best ideas for influencing His desires into the lives of people is a troubling notion at best. Nothing sucks the love out of love more than fear.

What if God wants me to kill myself? That's a question I seriously asked during my walk as a conservative Evangelical. I had been taught to be afraid of God, and my mind was simply taking it to its furthest conclusion. I am going to keep on sinning and falling short, that's for sure. So, why not just end it all, avoid God's punishment, and keep from disappointing Him so badly. My relationship with God is the most important thing, is it not? Besides, I could ask for forgiveness and then pull the trigger assured that I was free of any unrepentant sins that might disqualify my salvation. If hell is real, and God's forgiveness is conditioned by my repentance, suicide might be the most secure solution. Surely, God would rather have me dead with repentance than alive with disobedience. If you are going to believe that salvation is conditioned by human response, believe it all the way.

Thankfully, by the Grace of God, I recognized the deception and the spiritual war going on within. Yet sadly, many who are reading will not.

I used to live my life paranoid, afraid, and half-heartedly trusting in the conservative Evangelical god whose countenance toward me I could never be certain of, but, now, the Spirit of Jesus within me has convinced my heart, God is love—wholly, completely, and purely. He has nothing but affection for me and every human being. No condemnation, no punishment, no desire for revenge—He perfectly loves me with perfect consistency. All this fiery talk about hell, wrath, judgment, and God's discipline—it's not only all highly debatable and open to be differently interpreted, but all silenced at the foot of the cross. Captured by Jesus who adores humanity without limit or restriction, I refuse to live my life fearing, doubting, and in a constant state of paranoia over a conservatively-imaged god who could love me one moment and cast me into hell the next, simply because I don't love Him back in precisely all the right, "conservative" ways. Is God truly that impotent and codependent on humanity?

I'm not trying to leave you behind, but I just can't help but be determined to live my life seeing God through the lens of Jesus—perfecting me on the cross and perfectly loving me without conditions for eternity. For God is for me, whom shall I fear?

Yes, a life without fear, that's my longing and, thankfully, God's longing for me. I pray that you would see and feel it, too. Love and peace now fills the air since I've become convinced that God paces the halls of heaven looking for ways to bless me and assure me of His goodness. There is no more one-eyed open living for me; that's all been replaced by a one-hearted leaning on the God who is Love, completely and thoroughly.

Because His Grace is sufficient, I am always sufficient—there has never been nor will there ever be a time when I am not. This is the one and only revelation that has ever given rest to the restlessness of my heart, and, now, inoculates me from all fear, insecurities, doubt, condemnation, and shame. I cannot out-sin, out-fail, or out-cast the love of the Lover.

I'm sorry conservative Evangelical Christianity, I just can't do it anymore.

I Can't Ask My Wife To Submit To Me

Sadly, it's just a part of the conservative Evangelical code, often unwritten, that males are superior and spiritual maturity is found when one discerns that women are emotionally incapable of the levels of leadership needed for the home and church.

This is a mindset I once adopted and now deeply regret.

What a waste of sacred human divinity it is to conclude than any person is inferior, especially women. Yet, even worse, how dreadful and oppressing it is to live with that framework being the guide to your relational paths with people in general.

With all the ways God has created women equally, with the divine written into every fiber of their being, my soul tires of being summoned to dismiss women as lesser human beings by a male-driven, conservative Christianity that seems insistent on their sexist way of contextualizing and interpreting the Apostle Paul and his teachings. My wife and I are a team on completely equal footing—for that's what it means to be one flesh. Jesus speaks, equips, calls and empowers her in all the same ways He does with me—her potential in life, church, family, and ministry is no less than mine. She can do anything and everything with complete freedom in Christ. She is not weaker, less capable of leading, nor deserving of anything unequal because of her gender. I just want to live my life seeing my wife and all women as Jesus does—completely, thoroughly, and unequivocally equal in all things—period, full stop.

I'm sorry conservative Christianity, I just can't do it anymore.

I Can't Deny The Validity Of Science

Forcing a literal biblical understanding upon every aspect of an entire worldview, to me, is no longer honest or wisdom embracing. Demanding that the earth has an age of merely 6,000 years, evolution is fake news, and global warming is a myth, is to create a war of intellect, science, and common sense where there need not be. In both matters of the spiritual and scientific, our human capacity to fully comprehend, define, and know for certain is highly limited. Our faith would do well to simply conclude what is truly most important—God created and creates.

I just want to live my life with my brain turned on to the awareness that scientific discovery and spiritual revelation don't have to be enemies, but are important threads that are actually woven together in the great, divine tapestry of life. God is neither threatened, separate, nor necessarily contradictory to science and its discoveries—therefore, neither will I be.

I'm sorry conservative Christianity, I just can't do it anymore.

I Can't Turn Off My Brain, Deny My Individuality, And Freeze-Dry My Beliefs

It may have been a long time coming, but I've finally awakened to the costs that the controlling spirit that plaques so much of conservative Evangelical Christianity has had upon my life and those around me. How I ever swallowed the pill that insists that God desires my conformity to the conservative right-wing brand of Christian faith is beyond me.

If I'm honest, my heart now trembles at the evil in which I participated while leading people to believe that conformity is the goal of Christ in their lives. Reducing God and His desires to a set of beliefs, behaviors, conditions, and expectations is to worship an idol fashioned in our own image. How thoroughly deplorable a person I became every moment I manipulated people to march to the beat of the conservative Evangelical drum, eroding and eclipsing the true work of the Spirit in their lives. For when you don't trust the Spirit nor believe that God is greater than your agenda, you exert control because control is all you have. Sadly, a controlling spirit finds its crack cocaine in much of conservative Evangelicalism.

This is my experience and I can't deny it. The pure Gospel of Grace shook me and, soon, I realized that I'm on a spiritual journey, not at a destination. God gave me a brain with common sense and a conscience. I'm convinced that God's desire isn't that I land in a cold existence of conformity to a certain set of approved beliefs, but that I'm always growing in my awakening to His Grace—forever fluid to where that might take me emotionally, spiritually, physically, and confessionally. Jesus created me as a complicated, unique, divinely-loaded individual that should resist all human-born labels that would seek to limit, control, own, cage, or define me. Where conservative Christianity largely desires to assimilate and mold me, I just want to live my life enjoying the freedom for which Jesus freed me.

Imagine a landscape so eternally broad upon which you cannot travel outside of God's wisdom and His willingness to allow you the freedom to grow, think, feel, and forever consider His nature and ways. For Jesus is far less concerned about our conclusions than our having the trust in Him required to be able to question and even disbelieve.

I'm sorry conservative Christianity, I just can't do it anymore.

I Can't Believe The Bible Is Perfect

The sacred cow that rules the pastures of so much of conservative Evangelical Christianity has finally been tipped over inside of me. Grace has convinced me, nothing and no one is perfect but Jesus. He is the only Word of God, everything else is human words about God. Yes, they can be deemed as inspired, but never infallible—for aren't we all inspired by God anyway, with a story to tell and perspectives along the way? For how can you not be—He is ALL and in ALL things. Inspiration never guarantees accuracy.[43]

With a new way of seeing and believing, I'm tired of reducing the Bible to a playbook for living, debate-winning, and lording over my critics and those conservative Christianity deems to be sinning. I just want to live my life captivated by the mystery, experiences, and faith stories God uses in Scripture to lead me into a personal, life-long, and ever-expanding encounter with Jesus—progressively awakening to Him who is Grace.

I'm sorry conservative Christianity, I just can't do it anymore.

I Can't Compete With You And Your "Sold Out" Family

You're just too good, much too good for me. I'm not trying to be facetious, just honest.

In fact, I was the Christian and pastor who subscribed to and fostered competitive Christianity. Be all you can be for Jesus, make sure you're one step ahead of everyone else, and if all else fails, don't let anybody see that you're falling short and, maybe even, falling apart. For some, it's a bit more subtle, but nonetheless serious.

Yet, for all my efforts, even as a minister, you always surpassed me. I can't believe I played the Christian comparison game and let it dictate my self-talk. For the sure mantra of much of American Christianity is "enough is never enough."

With all the ways you say you are so "blessed," the religious art and knickknacks decorating your house, and the sheer height of your hands lifted up in worship, I simply can't keep up. For all the times you commit to people, "I'll be praying for you," I wonder how you have time for nearly

---

[43] Colossians 1:15-20; 1 Corinthians 15:28

anything else. Considering the never-ending litany of Facebook pictures of your highlighted Bible next to a coffee cup, scripture-quoting memes, and subtly self-congratulating celebrations of faithfulness, I have a hard time resisting the conclusion that there must be something wrong with me. You've got it going on with Jesus in so many ways that I simply don't and can't.

Yet, as much as it all seems so impressive, I just want to live my life outside the pressure and lifting-up of all that—stuff. You will always be more spiritual and faithful than me.

Finally, by the Grace of God, I'm learning to enjoy the joy that comes from being completely at peace with that. I don't have to live my life trying to keep good going and pretending when it's not. In fact, Jesus has made it clear that's not living at all, but, rather, a sure prescription for emotional and spiritual death.

I'm sorry conservative Christianity, I just can't do it anymore.

I Can't Love People Conditionally

I know you believe my sense of love is too soft, slippery, dangerous, and without teeth. Yet, the truth is, I just can't stomach it anymore. To think of all the people and relationships I poisoned with conditional love, makes my heart sick.

Besides, it takes so much work, judgment, reservation, and energy. Who is deserving, who is not? How much is too much, or just right? What's the perfect mix of conditions, clauses, and confronting? Where does one even begin in mixing a perfect love-with-conditions cocktail? When have they changed, repented, believed, and behaved enough to unlock the door to love or at least to let them peek in?

The truth is, Grace has shown me, that's not how Jesus loves me, nor anyone that has ever been or ever will be. In fact, He loves without restraint, conditions, restrictions, or fine print. I just want to live my life with the "love conditions" radar screen turned off, knowing and trusting my purpose and scope is to love people unconditionally, and let God untangle the rest. And if I err, I will boldly approach the throne of God having loved too much, if that ever could be a thing.

I'm sorry conservative Christianity, I just can't do it anymore.

I Can't Condemn The LGBTQ Community

I'm sorry, I just can't.

I can't ignore the real stories and journeys of the LGBTQ community, and the truth they bring to the table. I can't deny the faithful scholarship of Bible-loving, truth-seeking, Jesus-loving, and unbiased scholars who find no other alternative but to conclude that the Bible is actually affirming of LGBTQ people—as I do.

I can't condemn where there isn't certain certainty, but, rather, the sure potential that conservative Christianity could very well be completely wrong. With an undeniable history of wrongfully judging, disapproving, and damning things, later proven to be benign and even divine, I am learning to never lean on a conservative Christian understanding.

I just want to live my life outside of the condemning, discriminating, and sin-labeling mantra of conservative Christianity that shoots first and consults Jesus later—if at all.

I'm sorry conservative Christianity, I just can't do it anymore.

I Can't Embrace A Gospel That Is,
For Me, No Gospel At All

I'm a changed man who was once lost in a conservative Evangelical trance that only Grace could find its way through. I've tasted and seen that God is pure Love, and Jesus is all Grace, and, now, my soul won't let me consume nor settle for anything less—for to do so would be a blasphemy against the Spirit and His work in me. I believe the Apostle Paul was centered onto divine truth when He charged that a Gospel mixed with any level of Law, conditions, or human performance is in fact, no Gospel at all—even to a level of being accursed.[44]

I take sin so seriously that it is my deep confession and personal experience that no one can master, manage, nor overcome it, but Jesus, who is Grace. It is the Grace of God that empowers, teaches, and inspires us to divine change and right living—nothing else can or will.

The conservative Evangelical gospel filled with "to do" steps, conditions, rule-keeping, fear-living, and hell-requiring is to me, no Gospel at all, but, rather, a sure ministry of death. I just want to live my life truly living, because my heart has been overcome and irrevocably endeared to a Gospel that is nothing but Grace, life at its very best, and pure freedom.

It's not that I don't love you anymore—I do. It's not that I don't accept you without conditions—I do. It's not that I don't believe you are filled with good intention and tremendous, God-adorned worth and value—I do.

I'm sorry conservative Christianity, I just can't do it anymore.

---

[44] Galatians 1:6-9

"The most courageous act is still to think for yourself. Aloud."
—Coco Chanel

CHAPTER THIRTEEN
No Longer Afraid, Finding Life After

Perhaps, for you, you can't do it anymore, either. The doubts can no longer be contained, your heart can no longer be constricted, and your soul is no longer afraid. There's a bravery that Grace is welling up from within you. Maybe you don't have it all lined-up and your mind isn't thoroughly convinced, but something is happening within your soul that can no longer be denied.

This is the journey I have taken, having escaped the conservative Evangelical war on all things Jesus—only by His Grace. It hasn't been an easy road, the ramifications aren't always pleasant. However, the rewards are incomprehensible and priceless. Yet, now, the true work begins, as breaking the death grip of conservative Evangelicalism may be challenging, but this resurrection stuff can even be a bit more difficult.

Perhaps, you will close this book and largely dismiss it. Perhaps the wheels are turning in your mind and heart with a lot of questions. Perhaps, you're experiencing the onset of regret and repentance. Perhaps, a fresh wind of revelation and courage is filling your sails.

No matter who you are and where you are, it's not by chance that we have traveled through these pages.

Many are those who have been hurt and harmed by conservative Evangelical Christianity. A walk through the haunted woods of right-wing, religious America can be a painful, faith-stripping, and life-sucking experience. For some, it's an alarming set of events that must transpire before their eyes are opened to the religious deceptions and evils they have endured, adopted, or perhaps have even empowered. Many within and outside of conservative Evangelical Christianity can attest to the victim or victimizer they have become as a result of the faith and practices of much of religious right-wing America.

For those who have been deceived into befriending or becoming the religious evils of conservative Evangelical Christianity—there is hope. For those whose lives have been devastated, their faith disillusioned, and their dignities raped at the hands of these same religious evils—there is hope.

Raise your head, open your heart, awaken your soul—there is a sure and certain hope.

The time is now to unwrap from the burial clothes of conservative Evangelicalism, rise up from your baptism into Grace, and put on the bravery of new life, identity, fulfillment, and purpose.

Be who you are, fully, without apology or restraint.

There is so much to live for. There is so much to die for. There is so much to believe in.

The life you were created to live, and your soul has been begging for you to embrace, is before you.

There Is Grace Instead Of Conditions

Yes, it's true, there is a Gospel that is devoid of fiery judgment, religious condemnation, guilt-trips, "to-do" lists, love-prequalifying, and people-shaming. There is a Gospel where everyone is deemed equal, affirmed, included, and eternally loved and valued. There is a Gospel absent of an angry, vengeful God who requires the murder of His Son and the proper religious responses of His creation in order to forgive and save humanity. There is a Gospel where God loves unconditionally, because that's who He is and can do no other. There is a Gospel that stands against all violence, abuse, and idolatry, and, yet, in all these things, is no less biblical. This Gospel is not a fad, a new theology, or some wayward heresy—it's a person and that person is Jesus who is pure Grace.

For me, it began by listening. In one simple conversation, my longtime pastor and mentor admonished me to give ear to some preachers and teachers who were sharing the message of the pure Gospel of Grace. It had transformed his thinking, and he wondered if it might transform mine. At first, I was grossly offended and deemed it all to be blasphemy. Everything I held to be true was put into question. Yet, I kept on listening. In fact, for a couple hours a day, weeks-upon-weeks. The one thing I knew deep within my being was that the tenets of conservative Evangelicalism weren't working to truly make my life better, especially in the area of overcoming sin. Perhaps I was missing the answer, and this new revelation could reveal the remedy.

I say it again, it began by listening—turning down the conservative Evangelical echochamber reverberating in my head and listening.

I'm not sure of the exact moment, but there was certainly a kind of cosmic pause when the message finally clicked. Grace is the answer, and everything else isn't. It's hard to put into words, but my spirit was connected to the Truth it had long been seeking. I was breathing for the first time, and my soul was finally free.

I kept on listening, taking it further, as far as the streams of Grace would lead. Every strain of the religious spirit that imprisoned me was unraveling around my soul. The scales that once blinded me were removed, revealing the religious cancer that had plagued me for so long.

I was flabbergasted to see the lies I had been believing, and the evil person I had become—-broken down to my knees with regret and repentance. One thing I knew for sure, I was a new person, and there could be no turning back. Once you've tasted pure Grace, nothing else will do.

Soon, my relationship with my wife changed with a fresh new wind of joy and peace. She saw the transformation in me, bringing a new sense of freedom to her spirit. We have always had a great relationship, but the freedom to be fully ourselves, let down our hair, and enjoy life reached an all new level, blessing every aspect of our togetherness. No more policing of each other's spiritual lives, refraining from having too much fun, and living under the pressures of religious expectations and appearances. I was a completely different kind of friend to my friends, and parent to my children—everything looked different. The relational tool box of guilt-trips, spiritual-fruit inspection, religious rule-keeping, condemnation, lecturing, punishment, and score-keeping was relieved of its duties.

In fact, prior to this new level of Grace-awakening, we had been having a heightened level of difficulty with our son. Perhaps it was the pressures of high school or hating the town in which we live. Nonetheless, his increasing temper and bursts of rage were getting out of control. My conservative Evangelical grooming had led me to come up with the perfect solution, a long, written covenant of behavioral conditions that he would have to fulfill, making sure our expectations were perfectly clear. If he was complicit, good things would result. If not, the daunting consequences were sure. I sat him down, went over the contract, and sternly pasted it on the refrigerator door, just like any good conservative Evangelical would do.

Sure, it worked for a week or two as he followed the rules. But then, it eventually broke down and even got worse. It was during that same time that the message of pure Grace was starting to break through. One evening, with a fresh new heart and perspective, I summoned Harrison into the kitchen. I grasped the covenant off the refrigerator and tore in half, throwing it onto the floor. I told Harrison, there will be no more punishment, conditions, nor condemnation, "We love you, and that's the beginning and end of all that matters." I impressed upon him my sincere apologies for being such a grace-less dad, and asked for his forgiveness. He was free to choose the course of his behaviors, not out of fear of punishment or obligation to a set of rules, but because He is loved and deserves the blessings of choosing well. You could see the surprise in his eyes and a new countenance wash over him. I kid you not, from that day forward, his heart, attitude, and behavior forever changed for the better.

It's amazing what a little bit of listening will do, especially when what you are listening to is pure Grace--love without conditions.

When the sun shines now, it really shines. When the stars glisten now, they really glisten. When my children laugh, I can truly laugh with them. When my wife loves me, I can truly love me and truly love her in return. When there is joy in the room, I can truly tap into it. When I see people hurting, I can truly hurt with them. When I look at all humanity, I can finally see the divine affirmation in all of it. Not because I am better, but because Jesus has always been better in me.

If you want to experience Grace and be awakened in your soul, start listening and never stop—have the courage. Taste and keep on tasting, God is truly good, better than you could ever imagine.

When it comes to listening, here's a few questions that were important for me, and I hope will be helpful to you.

• In your mind and heart, what's it going to take for God's grace to be fully sufficient for you?

• What scares you the most about embracing the purity of God's grace for your life and the lives of others?

- How's all the lecturing, punishing, guilt-tripping, spiritual policing, and loving with conditions working for yourself and in your friendships, romantic relationships, and parenting?

There Is Jesus Outside Of Church

Yes, He lives, moves, and breathes outside of "church," and, dare I say, in many instances, more freely and powerfully.

It is perhaps one of the most subtle erosions that takes place in one's indoctrination and life within conservative Evangelical Christianity. The inward belief that Jesus grants special favor to white, male, heterosexual Evangelicals and is exclusively known by them in ways others cannot be, is a kind brainwashing that is hard to overcome.

The thought that Jesus exists fully and can be fully known outside of the Evangelical Borg of ministry, church, and conservative ideology, is highly unpopular among conservatives to even consider. In fact, it's nearly impossible to participate in conservative Evangelicalism without being led to believe that a church building is "God's house," church attendance is necessary for encountering God and being a genuine Christian, and becoming an active member of a "Bible believing" church is a required ingredient to spiritual maturity.

Yet, the eyes of Grace reveal that Jesus is alive and well outside of "church" as much (and perhaps even more) as He ever was within.

Have no fear, when nearly everything about American Christianity increasingly makes you want to vomit, it's not the Spirit that's leaving you, it's Grace that is awakening you. From Christian radio, to church growth tactics; from slick modern worship staging to cheesy Facebook posts of highlighted Bible verses; from optic mission trips to pretentious fellowships; from theological debates to spiritual navel gazing; and from celebrity pastors with cult followings to clever branding to seduce the masses. If it all makes you cringe and spit up in your mouth a bit, not only are you not alone, but perhaps the mind of Christ within you is finally being heard.

Unfortunately, this revelation is initially often met with sticky levels of guilt, shame, and anxiety. To not attend a church or be involved in some kind of "church" ministry, at first, feels weird and unclean. However, as the claws of religion lose their grip around our souls, we soon discover that the entire cosmos of God's creation is our sanctuary, we are walking Trinities with skin, and our worship is to simply love without conditions. The ultimate tribe we are seeking is within—Father, Son, Holy Spirit. We are the revival, we are the "big" thing God is doing. Ministry is anywhere and everywhere as we simply do what we love to do in ways that honor Grace. There is no perfect plan or specific purpose you are supposed to discover and live. You are God's perfect plan, and you being fully you is the purpose. Salvation has already come for all humanity, our job is to enjoy, live, and extend it--love for everyone everywhere, without conditions.

Yes, there is a Jesus who is everywhere and in all things. He is not exclusive to any one location, nation, group, orientation, gender, skin color, tradition, ideology, political party, or even faith system—He is all and in all, nowhere can He be found missing. He is not in public schools unless the people within them are praying or the Bible is being read. He can't be summoned, controlled, or enticed into favoritism. As much as one may encounter Him in Church, they can encounter Him anywhere and in all things—if they have ears to hear, eyes to see, and a heart that is willing. Jesus isn't just in Church or into Church people, nor a building, or a service—He's in everyone, everywhere, and everything. He's into all humanity.

It may just be, the more you open your life to Grace, the more you will feel compelled to follow Jesus out of much of church-driven American Christianity. You don't have to endure the pressures to conform, perform, and meet expectations. Jesus is fully willing and, perhaps, even prefers to meet you outside of all that. Besides, He already lives within you.

When it comes to experiencing Jesus outside of church, here's a few questions that were important for me, and I hope will be helpful to you.

- What does attending a church symbolize to you that, perhaps, makes you feel guilty or inauthentic as a Christian if you don't participate?

- Is there anything about church that has become a way for you to appease, please, or assure yourself that God will bless and take care of you?

- In your mind, what is there to fear in experiencing Jesus, serving people, and worshipping Him outside of a formal church experience?

There Is Community Beyond A Congregation

Yes, there is spiritual, Jesus-filled community outside of a formal congregation, and, dare I say, in many instances, more authentically.

The first time it happened in a profoundly recognizable way, Amy and I were sitting at the bar of one of our local pizza restaurants. Yes, we now enjoy the freedom to drink beer, especially the kind you can't see through. We had dined there often and built relationships with both the staff and people that frequently visited. No, the heavens didn't open, nor was there a worship band leading us in emotional songs of praise. Instead, in a beautiful moment of awareness, gathered together with normal people, laughing and loving, we realized we were in the presence of God and authentic community. Maybe, for the first time.

In all my years of ministry in the so-called Christian "community," I had never experienced the sense of warmth, ease, connection, and presence of Jesus more than in that moment, and many to follow.

When you begin to see people through the eyes of Grace, there is Jesus-flavored community everywhere, as far as the heart can see. Community is far less defined by the beliefs of the people you are with and much more defined by how you see them and yourself. Choosing authenticity over false community is a choice you'll never regret. For, if church is a place you go filled with people who believe and act as you, you'll never get there.

In fact, as opposed to church congregations that are largely organized around agreed beliefs, values, preferences and purpose, true community is found deeper where all beliefs are honored, love is most highly valued, and purpose is centered on mutual respect, compassion, and human service—diversity is prized, not feared. It's where people love, not out of religious obedience or faith obligation, but because it is who they are and the full essence and nature of the God they worship. No greater form of community is found than at the Jesus-table that extends far beyond the confines of many a congregation into the realm where people simply intersect with people—anytime, anywhere, and anyplace. The planet becomes our sanctuary, loving people become our worship service, and all humanity, our congregation—no one is excluded—no walls, windows, steeples, stages, logos, or carpets needed.

When it comes to experiencing community outside of a formal congregation, here's a few questions that were important for me, and I hope will be helpful to you.

- The root word for "evil" in the New Testament centers around the idea of a person striving to make a name for oneself, particularly in their relationship with God. With many churches embracing this same "evil" in their fellowships as they gather to put on their spiritual performances in an effort to draw closer to God, maintain their good standing, and get more Jesus in their life, why do we assume that having fellowship with the so-called "world" is darker than being in fellowship at a church?

- Is there something about being in a church community of like-believing, like-minded people that makes you feel that perhaps you're better than others, safer in your beliefs, and separate from having to interact with the world, other than to convert them into your community?

- When was the last time you could completely think, feel, and believe fully as yourself without fear, shame, or hesitation within a formal church congregation? Would you even know how to do that?

There Is Love Without Restriction Or Restraint

Yes, there is a love that is only love when it's given unconditionally, and you can experience the joyous bliss of extending it without fear and reservation. It's real, it's true, it's waiting for you.

Ever since the day Amy and I married, my relationship with my in-laws had been strenuous at best. Looking back, I am sure a good portion of it was fueled by our insecurities, for when you are a faithful conservative Evangelical, there is much to be insecure about. Yet, there were also significant levels of legitimate concern. What began as conflicts with Amy's parents spilled over to her entire family. Every visit was filled with stress and awkwardness. For years and years, we sought to navigate these tensions, but were never successful in doing so. Our conservative Evangelical methods of setting strong boundaries, punishing with consequences, and believing we were spiritually justified in disconnecting from the family never worked. It was then that we decided on a different approach as Amy's family became our project. We concluded that if there was ever going to be family peace, it would be because we "discipled" them and got them truly "saved" (even though they were already professing Christians). In fact, during one Christmas, we purchased all of our family members a copy of the book, "23 Minutes In Hell," thinking that would get the ball rolling. I can still see their eyes of disbelief and shock upon unwrapping each one. Needless to say, for all of our conversion efforts, none of it worked. With every month, the distance and animosity grew. That is, until we finally awakened to Grace.

Grace was changing everything about us, and it was time we applied it to Amy's parents and family. For the first time in 18 years, we sat with her mom and dad around the dinner table at their summer home to discuss the tensions that had long been existent between us. Aware of the damage our pretentious conservative religiosity had long been causing, we communicated our repentance and regret. They, too, owned their own faults along the away. As Grace filled the room, we began to see each other, no longer as enemies that can hurt each other, but people who love and that we deeply loved. A new sense of perspective, understanding, and mutual affection enveloped the room. We could love them without restraint or restriction—Grace had come. Our defenses were dismantled, and new life emerged. If only Grace had been in our hearts sooner, negating all those years wasted in unnecessary animosity and distance.

Remember the lesbian woman I introduced to you in an earlier chapter who began to change my entire perspective on human sexuality and God's heart towards it? For so long, my conservative Evangelical faith required me to pump the breaks on loving her, and to make sure I kept a safe distance. Any bit of love that I might send her way must be packaged with conditions and restrictions, lest she be led astray.

Yet, I'll never forget the moment. It felt like the heavens did open this time when I realized I could love her without restraint or restriction, my heart was finally free. I knew in that moment, in a way like never before, that Jesus truly lived within me. For no one loves like Jesus until they love without conditions, restrictions, or restraints.

Isn't this what your heart has been longing for, to feel the full force of Jesus living through you?

No more sizing people up or pre-qualifying expressions of Grace. No more wondering and fearing that you could love too much—if that ever could be a thing. No more conditions, fine-print, or exemptions. No more relational distancing out of religious obligations. No more "hate the sin, love the sinner" in order to desensitize your soul and justify condemnation and hate. No more saying "no" when everything in your spirit is saying "yes." No more separating "truth" and "love" because your heart has been awakened to the revelation "the Truth is Love, and Love is the Truth"—one in the same of the blessed Trinity. No more holding back, shrinking back, or turning back—only giving back as God has first given love to you—without restriction or restraint.

When it comes to experiencing and expressing love without restriction or restraint, here's a few questions that were important for me that I hope will be helpful to you.

- What scares you most about loving people in ways that present zero conditions attached?

- If God doesn't love people unconditionally, how can we ever know for sure that His conditions have been met without ultimately trusting something within ourselves more than in Him?

- What has the cost been in your life in waiting for and requiring people to fulfill your expectations before extending them unconditional love, pure grace, and unmerited forgiveness?

There Is Freedom Above Conformity

Yes, there is a freedom to be fully you without apology or shame. Not just a freedom, but a mandate from the heavens above. You don't owe anyone an explanation, verse, or justification. The days of engaging in competitive Christianity and striving to be the lead scorer in the comparison game can finally be over.

Break the chains of control and manipulation that have long eclipsed your beauty. God is for you, not against you. He delights in everything about you, not because you don't miss the mark from time-to-time, but because His love never does.

In truth, you have no one to fear. God perfectly loves you and embraces you completely. He affirms you no less than His gaze into a mirror—you are the image of the Divine Creator. Your value and worth have been predetermined and made forever certain. His love, approval, and acceptance are irrevocable and unchanging. That He created you is more than reason enough to hug you with an embrace that is eternally unbreakable. No one's opinion, voice, declaration, proof-text, or sermon should even begin to matter compared to the ultimate statement of God on your behalf, "It is finished." God's love for you—done deal. God's delight in you—done deal. God's affirmation of you—done deal. God's salvation for you—done deal. As is, whoever you are. All is Grace, one and done—you are an unstoppable force of the Father. You are the revival God is bringing to the earth.

That's why Jesus didn't come to set you free only for conservative Evangelicalism to imprison you with their tractor beams of guilt, shame, and religious rule-keeping. For right-wing, conservative Christianity knows that without "control" they have nothing—that's the very essence upon which their entire faith system hinges.

Thankfully, God didn't create you to be controlled, He created you to be free. Free to live, free to be loved, and free to love in return.[45]

In fact, Grace gives you the full freedom to sin. Yes, that's right, Grace gives you the full freedom to sin. In fact, if you don't feel the full freedom to sin, you haven't felt the full freedom of the Gospel.

---

[45] John 8:32, 36

See, because here's what conservative Evangelicalism doesn't want you to know. It is only in that full freedom to sin that sin finally loses its appeal and stronghold upon our heart—writing the conclusion in our soul "I could, but I don't want to" for all the right reasons. That's why Grace is the only "Teacher" whose class is worth attending and whose prescription for life and living is the only one worth taking. You are free, completely—class dismissed.

For there is a spiritual growth that knows no limits and has no bounds. The goal is not conformity to a set of beliefs and convictions, but effortlessly becoming all that you already are by the Grace of Jesus. It's founded on a trust and declaration that God is bigger than our best thoughts, ideas, conclusions, behaviors, and confessions. His desire is not that we land in a place of determined theological correctness, but that we open our sails to the Spirit to take us wherever Grace might lead us. That we listen to His voice speaking with fresh revelation fills His heart with delight far more than to see our heads buried in pages and verses. You are a free-living, free-thinking, free-aspiring creation, and God loves to see you embracing freedom fully.

With bravery, be you, fully you. Live your life doing what you love to do in ways that honor God who is Love.

When it comes to experiencing freedom from religious conformity, here's a few questions that were important for me, and I hope will be helpful for you.

- If God created you to be you (which He did), but you aren't willing to be you, then why did God create you in the first place?

- If true spiritual growth isn't about becoming something tomorrow that you aren't today, but instead about becoming more fully who you already are in Christ, how does that change your approach to yourself and finding freedom within?

- Does God truly desire for you to conform to the interpretations of a book by people who can't even agree upon issues as central as salvation? Are there higher standards toward which we are to trim our sails?

There Is Forgiveness For The Enemy

Yes, there is the divine capacity to never become the evil done against us. It begins and ends with forgiveness.

There will always be people who will stand against a God who is pure Love, your divine affirmation, and His unconditional love and inclusion of all humanity. This can be an extremely painful and oppressive reality that can leave lasting scars. However, to drink from the cauldron of unforgiveness is to consume the poison, not the cure. No, forgiveness doesn't mean that wrongs become magically right and relationships are automatically restored. Yet, it does mean, no one is discarded and deemed unredeemable and unworthy.

When we choose the path of forgiveness, taking the high road and living to love again is not only the cry of our soul, but the empowerment we become—free from all that is religious. It's then that we achieve the beautiful balance of standing firm to our truth while avoiding becoming the evil done against us. No longer can one drag us into meaninglessness nor bring out in us a person foreign to grace and graciousness.

In fact, even the worst of that which is done against us is gleaned of its lessons but neutered of its power to possess. Confronted by and collided with a forgiveness that is unlimited, compels us to free ourselves from the shackles of unforgiveness, that we might never become our own worst enemy. What the evils of religion have stolen from us will become our mandate to no longer give them headspace nor power through being imprisoned to their hate.

It is then that we become determined to refuse to hold onto bitterness, the desire for revenge, or the expectation of change. Those who forgive freely are those who are truly free and show themselves to be fully rescued out of the shadows of conservative Evangelical Christianity.

Yet, perhaps, the hardest form of forgiveness is to give it to oneself. Detoxing from the conservative Evangelical system of faith can be filled with self-awareness that leaves us with deep levels of guilt and regret. This was certainly the case for me, but a common phrase helped to remind me of the Grace this journey affords, "It's not when a flower blooms that is most important, what's most important is that it blooms." Forgiving oneself is the final petal to blossom on the flower of your soul's awakening to Grace.

When it comes to extending forgiveness to yourself and others, here's a few questions that were important for me, and I hope will be helpful for you.

- If God has forgiven you (which He has), why haven't you?

- What does goodness or justice become for anyone who harbors bitterness and withholds forgiveness from oneself or others?

- How is your unforgiveness putting Jesus back on the cross and yourself on the throne?

- How can any relationship survive and rise above the capacity of the people involved to forgive?

Finding Purpose In The Pain

His name is Patrick, he had long adopted much of the tenets of conservative Evangelicalism over the course of his life. One year, just before Christmas, one of his relatives not only revealed her lesbianism, but, also, her plans to marry. For some time, he had distanced himself from her, having suspicions of her sexuality. Yet, something inside of him was becoming increasingly unsettled about harboring such condemnation toward her in his heart. It was then that he came across an article I had written on my website that described my painful spiritual journey away from conservative Evangelicalism and my affirmation of the LGBTQ community. In a matter of moments, his soul was broken wide-open and Grace awakened his heart. With a deep sense of regret and repentance, he soon realized just how much the Spirit of Jesus had been squelched in his life by right-wing religious conservatism. With a new perspective and a heart collided by Grace, he determined to not only attend the marriage ceremony, but to bless them with an extravagant gift, no matter how unpopular his actions might be received by others in his family. Today, he is not only a strong voice for the message of the pure Gospel of Grace, but a valued ally for the LGBTQ community. By the Grace of God, he is no longer afraid, and is finding purpose in the pain.

Her name is Tracy, she is Transgender. Upon the revealing of her truth, her family abandoned her and the church of her childhood swiftly rejected her, labeling her a disgusting abomination to God. Most of her friends soon left her side, and her faith in God was all but lost. One evening, she called me, having read an article and found my contact information. Her voice was shaking with a desire to end her own life. As we talked, she realized that she was not alone and that God deeply loves and affirms her. With an emerging calmness in her voice, she began to see a hope rising up from what had looked like a dark horizon of doom. For some weeks, we continued to talk, and today she is not only nearly complete with her transition, but active in a church working with young people to help build tolerance and respect for all of God's creation, no matter how seemingly different. By the grace of God, she is no longer afraid, and is finding purpose in the pain.

His name is Matt, he grew up in a Christian home with loving parents. Yet, later in his spiritual journey, the hypocrisy, elitism, and hate he witnessed being extended into the world by primarily conservative expressions of Christianity, called into question the entirety of his faith. With emotional, theological, and intellectual doubts building in his core, he decided the most honest alternative was to become an Atheist. Having been connected by a friend, he was curious about my spiritual journey, and how I still remained a Christian. Over the course of some deep conversations, he asserted that if there had been more people who held the same views and heart as I, he might not have ever jettisoned his faith in Christ. Today, Matt is still an Atheist, but sitting at the table of conversation where mutual respect and appreciation abounds. He is still interested in Jesus with an open mind. Most of all, he is convinced that if there is a God, He is big enough to handle the journey of his beliefs. He is no longer afraid, and is finding purpose in the pain.

Her name is Sarah, she loves Jesus and had been a life-long member of a church. She deeply valued the fellowship she often experienced and serving in her community. To walk away from her local congregation was the last thing she ever thought would occur, but with all she saw happening within much of American Christianity she felt like there was no other choice. At the end of the day, she tired of seeing politics, budgets, ideologies, programs, and doctrine become far more important than people. Perhaps, it was the moment when her pastor questioned her financial giving and the integrity of her faithfulness. Or, maybe it was the disapproval she witnessed in other church members when her white daughter decided to date a black man, and even get married. Over the course of time, with each issue that ensued, she concluded that "church" was no longer for her. With tremendous guilt and hesitation, she finally made the choice to walk away, and to walk away for good. At least until that day comes when, perhaps, a healthy church in her area emerged. Feeling like a fish flopping on the shores of a pond, at first, she was extremely uncomfortable without, seemingly, any path for her spirituality. However, in time she discovered a deeper sense of closeness with Jesus and community with people like never before, simply by looking for the sacred in everything and letting that be the track upon which her faith grows. Today, she is loving Jesus, people, and all of life with a renewed spirit. By the Grace of God, she is no longer afraid, and is finding purpose in the pain.

These are just a few of the countless stories of people who are escaping the conservative Evangelical war on all things Jesus. By the Grace of God, this could be your story, too.

For the person who has been caught up in the conservative Evangelical system of faith who is searching for answers, asking the tough questions, and even reconsidering their long-held beliefs, there is purpose in the pain.

For the parents who lay sleepless at night, fearing for the life and future of their LGBTQ child in a country filled with spiritually-rationalized bigotry and hate, there is purpose in the pain.

For the transgender person who carries the constant weight of religious oppression, discrimination, and demonization, there is purpose in the pain.

For the minorities that are exploited, abused, and deemed as lesser humans by much of society, there is purpose in the pain.

For the person sent to the curb by their local church for failing to meet expectations and submit to their calls for compliance, there is purpose in the pain.

For the pastor who is exercising a new-found bravery to stand up against the evils of conservative Evangelicalism, there is purpose in the pain.

For the unconditionally-loving Jesus among us and in us that is the constant target of conservative Evangelicalism and its war on Grace, there is purpose in the pain.

Leatherbound **Terrorism**

For the misfit who doesn't fit in,

For the victim who fears another day,

For the discouraged who struggle to find a way,

For the accused who have long been misunderstood and shamed, and

For the voiceless who long for the strength and the words for their song to be sung and their cries to be heard,

There is purpose in the pain.

Standing, resisting, crying out in fierce solidarity; giving voice to the voiceless, listening where no ears have been willing; defending and proclaiming the sacred value of all the discarded; living with a bravery of epic proportions that only a heart captured by Grace could compel; shouting for equality where there is none; ranting for justice where there is none; and chasing evils out of their shadows where they have long resided unchallenged.

These are the places where one finds the deepest purpose in life—to be fully yourself and fight on behalf of those who know not that joy. Taking the pain of your oppression and the story of your plight that it might empower another to overcome and discover true life.

You are the revival God is bringing to the world.

You are the star shining in the sky to light up a world blanketed by religious darkness.

You are the revelation of Jesus ushering in an awakening of the world to Grace.

You are the hope, you are the sacred, you are the eraser God is using to erase hatred.

Be no longer afraid.

Don't give up.

Don't give in.

There is always hope.

There is always the awakening to a new day and a new way.

In a world where much of conservative Evangelical Christianity shows little restraint in crucifying all that is truly divine, hear the call of Jesus upon your life, "Take up your resistance and follow me."

Grace is brave. Be brave.

Afterword:

My Apology

A person is not responsible for what they have been taught, but they are certainly responsible for what they believe and the ramifications thereof.

Along the conservative Evangelical path I had once taken, there are many rivers in which to cast the stones of blame, but, in the end, the ground reveals its truth, every footstep was ultimately my choice, for better or for worse. Many are the fossils of regret that can never be undone that reveal a history whose tales of tragedy will long endure.

To my wife, Amy: Words cannot express the depth of my sorrow when faced with the reality that, for so long, our lives were preoccupied with the allures of conservative Evangelicalism and my selfish desire to create my own personal ministry empire. You have selflessly sacrificed and suffered much, with a loyalty and patience that is beyond divine. My heart overflows with tears for all the burdens you have carried, and the time that has been wasted worshipping all that is religious. With every twist and turn, you have extended yourself graciously and always inspired me to be a better person. Together, we have weathered the incomprehensible, and, yet, become much in return. For that, I am grateful, but deeply saddened and filled with regret for the journey you endured.

To my son, Harrison: If only I had broken the cycle sooner. The father you have, now, is not the father I once was. Sadly, the faith system that poisoned my heart, bled unto you. To think of all the guilt, shame, condemnation, and conditional love I piled on top of your soul, fills my heart with deep remorse. Distracted by my selfish religious pursuits, I missed showing up for much of your childhood with the grace, patience, and connection you deserved. I am so very sorry.

Leatherbound **Terrorism**

To my daughters, Cailyn, Madelyn, and Ashton: Someday, when you read this, it may be hard to fully understand. The laughter, joy, compassion, freedom, grace, faith, and love that we now enjoy so thoroughly as a family will be given their context in a way that I hope fills your heart with deep appreciation and important lessons. That your little hearts have seen and heard the darkness I was, before my awakening to the Light, is a reality for which I am forever sorry.

To the churches I have pastored: My heart overflows with awful regret for all the ways I misled you into a false faith that was absent of Jesus, who is Grace, and, instead, overcome with the religious spirit. To each of you who I used for the purpose of building a ministry empire and medicating my insecurities, I am sorry. For all the times I filled your heart with fear, condemnation, and guilt, I am sorry. My misrepresentations of God and the Gospel were deplorable, at best. The blood of your disillusionment, deception, and doubts stain my hands. Where I meant to free you, I imprisoned you. This is to my forever shame and remorse.

To the black community: I can only kneel at your feet for forgiving and embracing me, a former racist. Where once I joined in the common chorus of discrimination, it is my honor to call you brother/sister and to stand alongside in solidarity. I am deeply sorry for every thought, word, and deed that sought to steal from you what truly can't be taken, your equal, divine value, worth, and dignity as fellow humans.

To my LGBTQ friends: You have my heart and my emboldened defense, yet, tragically, that has not always been so. I am so deeply sorry for every homophobic and transphobic attitude and belief I ever harbored against you. To think of the many ways I portrayed God as condemning you and despising your sexuality, strangles my soul with shame and regret. I am so sorry.

To all those whom my leatherbound terrorism has afflicted, I am sorry beyond what words can adequately express.

Thankfully, the conservative Evangelical system that once resided within me has been dismantled and the cycle broken. Please forgive me for the person I wasn't and for the person I was.

Today is a new day, filled with a new way. I hope it will be for us, too.

Grace is brave. Be brave.

Share your stories of crucifixion by
conservative Evangelicalism
and/or resurrection by Jesus at:

www.chriskratzer.com

You can privately connect
with the author at:

leatherboundterrorism@gmail.com

Made in the USA
San Bernardino, CA
25 June 2019